OUTSIDE PASSAGE

OUTSIDE
PASSAGE

A Memoir of an Alaskan Childhood

JULIA SCULLY

Random House

New York

Grateful acknowledgment is made to the Estate of Robert
Service c/o William Krasilovsky, as agent, for permission
to reprint eight lines of "The Cremation of Sam McGee" from
The Spell of the Yukon and Other Verses by Robert Service.
Reprinted by permission of the Estate of Robert Service c/o
William Krasilovsky, as agent.

Library of Congress Cataloging-in-Publication Data
Scully, Julia.
Outside passage : a memoir of an Alaskan childhood / Julia Scully.
— 1st ed.
p. cm.
ISBN 0-375-50083-9 (acid-free paper)
1. Scully, Julia—Childhood and youth. 2. Alaska—Biography.
I. Title.
CT275.S397A3   1998   979.8´04´092—dc21   97-34449
[B]

Random House website address: www.randomhouse.com
Printed in the United States of America on acid-free paper
98765432
First Edition

Book design by J. K. Lambert

For my sister, Lillian,
and in memory of Rose Hohenstein Silverman

Author's Note

This story is true to the best of my memory. But memory is flawed and colored by emotion and the events of the intervening years. Therefore, there may be some who might remember particular details, characters, and events differently.

While all of the people I have mentioned did exist, I have changed the names of many in order to avoid pain or embarrassment to them or their survivors.

Acknowledgments

My deepest gratitude to my friends and family—some of whom have helped me directly through suggestions and comments, and all of whom have sustained me with their consistent and loving support. This book wouldn't have happened without you.

Thanks, too, to my wonderful agent and friend, Martha Millard, and to Daniel Menaker at Random House—I couldn't have asked for a more enthusiastic, perceptive, and caring editor.

OUTSIDE PASSAGE

ONE

There wasn't a single tree in Nome. There wasn't a road that connected it to any other village or town. It would take you ten days to get there from Seattle on the Outside Passage—a rough voyage on the open sea with one landfall at the tip of the Aleutian Islands.

You could walk the entire town in five minutes. Well, maybe ten. Except for the Sand Spit. But there was nothing on that narrow stretch of sand beyond the jetty anyway, nothing but a few Eskimo hovels. About half of Nome's population of some 1,800 was Eskimo, or part-Eskimo—called "half-breeds" or "quarter-breeds." By and large, the whites looked on the natives as backward children.

If you walked to the northern edge of town, you came to the tundra—a brown, treeless, barren expanse. If you reversed yourself and went as far as you could in the opposite direction, you found Front Street and, just beyond it, the Bering Sea. Siberia was 200 miles away.

Except for Front Street, none of the streets in Nome had names. Or, if they did, no one knew them. There was one paved sidewalk, the one around the Federal Building, the three-winged, concrete centerpiece of Front Street that housed the post office, the court, the jail, and the land office where you went to stake a claim. The other sidewalks, when they existed, were wooden planks. The streets were mud in the summer, hard-packed snow in the winter.

The houses and the stores were little more than shacks clinging to the edge of the Bering Sea. Every fall there'd be a big storm, with the waves sometimes breaking over the buildings along Front Street, washing them out to sea or smashing them so that they lay on the ground like so many discarded toothpicks. Soon after, the ice pack drifted in from the Arctic, closing off the Bering Sea, and then it was silent, still, and white as far as the horizon and beyond. There followed seven long months of winter with the wind howling off the tundra, sweeping across the treeless outpost, whipping the snow into drifts that sometimes covered the houses, so that you had to shovel your way out.

The clear days were worse than the stormy ones. The ice crystals hung in the frigid air, stinging your chin, your cheeks, your nose, leaving them numb. You tried to keep your mouth closed, to shut out the freezing air. On such days there was hardly a soul on Front Street, although the Eskimos stood around sometimes in their parkas and mukluks, not seeming to notice that it was twenty below zero.

If you made the mistake of dying during the winter, you had to wait until spring to get buried.

The town had no sewer, no sanitation department. Unless you counted Eli the Scavenger. Eli poured the contents of the euphemistically named "chemical toilets" into an open, horse-drawn wagon. The stench of that wagon hung in the air and clung to your clothes after he passed. When he made his twice-weekly collections at your house, his own stink lingered for hours.

By spring, the snowdrifts, sometimes higher than a man's head, were black with soot from the oil smoke and dotted with dog droppings from the malamutes who roamed the streets in packs. Only a few people kept teams anymore, so there was no use for the animals.

Everyone in Nome looked forward to the "breakup" in the spring, when the ice would drift back to sea. It seemed to happen overnight. You looked out the window one morning and, instead of the momentously still white landscape, you'd see only small pieces of drifting ice now helplessly tossed and pounded by the turbulent water. Then everyone waited and watched every day, stopping on their errands to peer between the buildings on Front Street toward the horizon, looking for the First Boat to pull into the roadstead.

The First Boat that would bring clothes and furniture from Sears, Roebuck and Montgomery Ward, machinery for the gold-mining camps, a few precious cartons of fresh fruit and vegetables after months of nothing but canned, supplies for the stores on Front Street. And passengers—

men arriving for seasonal work at the gold-mining camps, women and children returning from a winter Outside in Seattle, or in Bellingham or Walla Walla, rejoining fathers and husbands whose work had required them to stay on, stay on through the long, brutal winter. And a few Cheechakos—the Alaskan's term for newcomers.

In the spring of 1940 my sister, Lillian, who was thirteen, and I, who was eleven, arrived alone on the First Boat to Nome.

TWO

Our journey to Nome began, you might say, on a day four years earlier in San Francisco. It was a brilliant October afternoon, glistening with the dazzling light peculiar to that city—a light that etched the edges of the shabby white apartment houses, creating sharp white lines against the cloudless blue sky, and caused the mica in the sidewalk to flash in our eyes as my sister and I made our way up Sutter Street on our way home from school.

We crossed wide Van Ness Avenue, a boulevard of automobile showrooms beyond which Sutter took a sharp rise. We might have stopped in the little bakery, where we sometimes bought a chocolate éclair to split between us. I can remember the way the warm chocolate icing melted into the whipped cream in my mouth. But perhaps we didn't have the dime that day and continued up Sutter past Butterworth & Butterworth, the auction house, where a fragile chair sat in the window like an actor on a stage, framed by an arch of velvet curtains. On past the small, three-story apartment houses such as the one in which we lived, round the corner to the dark shadows of Franklin Street, where our mom and dad had a coffee shop.

This was just the most recent of a series of failed coffee shops, ice-cream parlors, and delicatessens with which my parents had tried to make a living there in San Francisco. But it was 1936, the middle of the Depression, and no matter how hard they worked, they couldn't get by on selling a cup of coffee and a piece of pie for fifteen cents.

As soon as we reached the shop, my mother told us to run around the corner to the apartment and see if our dad was home. She'd been handling the place by herself all afternoon, waiting for him to get back from seeing the doctor.

I remember how dark it was in the front hallway, coming in from that brilliant sunshine. And that our feet made no sound on the carpeted stairway. And I remember that Lillian opened the door to the apartment and it was so quiet that I thought my father wasn't there. I rushed past her to get to the bathroom at the end of the hall and saw, for an instant, an image that remains imprinted in my mind. Through the open kitchen doorway I saw my father's wooden leg propped against the wall, its network of attaching straps dangling uselessly.

I don't know what happened next or even if I saw my father there on the kitchen floor. I just remember my sister and me running back down those silent stairs, running out into the blinding San Francisco sunlight, back to the coffee shop, back to my mother, who didn't need to ask what we had found.

THREE

Nothing is said about how my father died, or even, in fact, that he is dead. He just disappeared, and I wasn't really sure that he had ever been there in the first place.

Did I remember him? Did I remember the scratchy feel of his cheek when I leaned over the front seat of a car and rubbed my face against his? Did I remember when he laughed and took his pipe from his mouth and put it in mine? And did I remember the biting, bitter sting of it, that pipe on my tongue?

Did I remember climbing onto his lap, begging him to tell me a story, and him, in his long underwear, laughing and saying all right, here's the longest story in the world, and it was about a baby bird that grew so tired flying that it fell into a muddy place and got stuck, but was able to pull one leg out of the mud; but then it had to put that leg down to pull out the other leg and then the first leg was stuck, so it would put the second leg down to pull out the first leg, and then that was stuck and so the story never ended, because it is still in the mud to this very day, that baby bird, pulling out one leg and then the other.

My mother never mentions him. We don't go to the funeral, nor do we know what has happened to his remains. Still, there she is, in a black dress, sitting on a couch in a strange apartment with her head in her hands, crying.

Whose apartment is this? It belongs to friends of my parents, surely, and I know we are here because we can't go back to the place where something terrible has happened, but in my memory no one else is there—only my mother, my sister, and me.

And that very night, in that strange apartment, in a small room just big enough for the bed in which the three of us are sleeping, where a yellow light makes a blurry circle behind the tan shade on the window, I wake, sit up clutching my chest, knowing, with absolute certainty, that I have been shot.

And I hear my mother's weary voice saying, "It's just a dream. Go back to sleep."

Still, I remember, I do. Remember a long time ago, when we lived, all four of us, in the room in back of the Model Café on Polk Street. There was a patch of dirt out back, behind the room, and nasturtiums grew there, and I would bite the ends off the little horns that hung beneath the petals and suck out the drops of honey.

And I remember that, though I never got punished, this one day I did—I was lying in bed in the middle of the afternoon, sent to bed in the middle of the day, because I let the water run over in the bathroom and I am crying, alone in the bed, and my father comes in wearing a short white serving jacket. (Or do I just remember that jacket from a photograph, a photograph taken outside the Model Café, the name right there on the window, where he stands in that white serving jacket with those terrible, tortured eyes?) Still, I remember lying in that bed and crying and him sitting on the edge of the bed and pulling me up into his arms, and I'm looking up at his face, and I see that he is crying, too.

*

After my father dies, we don't go back to the apartment with the long hall with the kitchen on the right. We have a new apartment. It's on Sutter Street, too, but it's smaller—just one room with a kitchen and a bathroom. In the kitchen the table folds up into the wall and so does the ironing board. In the other room, the bed folds up into a door and the door swivels around and becomes a mirror. Lillian and I sleep in the Murphy bed and Mother sleeps on a couch under the window.

Mother doesn't work at the coffee shop around the corner on Franklin anymore. She works all the way downtown on Market Street, in a restaurant and bar called the Chevy Chase. When she comes home, it's after dark.

There is a trunk in that apartment and when I lift the top, it smells of some other place, a place very different from here, from this apartment on Sutter Street. And in it there is a photograph album with a crinkled leather cover. In the long hours after school, when my sister and I are alone, I go over and over the pictures in that album. And then the pictures become my memories.

Some are of my father, and they are from a long, long time ago. From when he was in Alaska, before I even knew him, before my mother even knew him. How handsome he was. Standing there all alone, dark against the white snow, wearing tall fur boots and a fur hat, a hunting knife strapped below his waist. How handsome and strong and unafraid he was. I remember my father was.

When it starts to get dark and the streetlights come on in the alley outside our apartment, I close the trunk and kneel on the couch looking out the window, waiting for Mother to come home. But I can't see anything except the alley with its garage doors all closed and blank, lit by the yellow light from the street lamps. Sometimes, then, I start to cry. Not because I want to. But because it's dark and there's nobody but Lillian and me in that little apartment and I don't know when my mother is coming home. My sister keeps telling me that she will be back soon, but I don't know when *soon* is.

When she does come home, carrying a towel-covered plate of lukewarm stew from the restaurant, her face is flushed above her white uniform and her ankles are swollen and she sinks into the big chair by the couch.

I climb into her lap and put my face against her cheek and smell the sweet odor of her face powder and the stale scent of cooking grease.

"*Kleine maideleh,*" she says. "*Kleine maideleh.*"

FOUR

My mother wasn't a pretty woman. But she was small and trim, smiled easily, and liked to laugh. Her only vanities were her small, well-shaped hands and feet.

She wore a full corset that laced up the front. And, over that, bloomers. When she took off her corset, her belly was creased from the stays and she would scratch herself in relief.

Her eyes were gray, the irises flecked with brown. She wore rimless glasses and had a tiny screwdriver to tighten the screws when they got loose.

She didn't raise her voice or argue. She said it was "common" to do that. Her anger was cold and took the form of silence and withdrawal.

The only time I saw her cry was the day of my father's funeral.

Although she was an immigrant with only a fourth-grade education, she thought herself as good as anybody. She loved America, was a naturalized citizen and proud of it.

Her name was Rose.

I know little of her early years. I do know that she was born in 1898, in what was then called Austria-Hungary, later Poland, in a village named Rohatyn. She and her twin sister were the last-born of a family of ten. Her twin died in infancy, as did three of the other children.

Shortly after Rose was born, her father left for America, taking with him the three oldest children. The plan was to send for the rest of the family as soon as he could find a livelihood. But he died in the new land, stranding the three children and leaving his wife alone to care for the rest. What happened to those in America—who took care of them and how they came to be separated one from the other—I never knew. What I do know is that my mother grew up in Rohatyn, that her family was poor, and that, at ten, she was taken out of school to clerk in a bookstore.

Still, her recollections of those times were of jokes and laughter. She had a sweet voice, and when she would stand outside her house singing, she told me proudly, people passing by sometimes gave her money.

As for Rose's mother, the grandmother I never met, I feel I saw a glimpse of her reflected in my mother's personality: resourceful, full of humor, deeply stoic.

Their little village became a battlefield during World War I. Soldiers fired rifles from the windows of their house. Rose's mother wouldn't let the children lie down in bed, fearing the devil would snatch their souls if they were killed while they slept. And after the fighting, Rose and her brother and sister were sent out to scavenge, searching for anything that might be traded for food. She remembered pulling the fine leather boots off dead Russian soldiers.

In 1921, when my mother was twenty-three, her oldest brother, Barney, sent her a ticket to come to the United States. Why she had been chosen over the others, she never said. But she came, speaking not a word of English. Or, rather, she learned three words to help her through the trip. I found them written in pencil in her familiar, careful little hand—*Pikel, Eiskrem, Patete*—on the elegant cover of the passenger list of the "RMS *Imperator* sailing from Southampton to New York (Via Cherbourg) Saturday, 8th January, 1921." And I remembered her story of how she had eaten several meals of pickles, ice cream, and potatoes in the ship's grand dining room before the waiter understood and took it upon himself to vary her menu. Her brother had been generous. She didn't travel steerage. She is listed as "Miss R. Einstoss," under "Second Cabin Passengers."

In Savannah, Barney, who had become successful managing a string of movie houses, arranged a job for her at a department store. If I can believe another of my mother's sometimes puzzling, sometimes hilarious recollections, her job was to man the information booth, although she spoke practically no English.

Whether it was that job, or the heat, or something else, Savannah didn't match up with Rose's notion of America, and she headed out to Seattle, where her sister, Sadie, lived with her husband and five children.

Rose found work in the fruit orchards of Washington. My sense of that time in my mother's life comes mainly from photographs. They reveal a lively, slim young woman with dark hair and bangs, invariably grinning at the camera. Wearing breeches and boots, she stands in front of the fruit trees, her arms around the shoulders of other young women who, like her, have lined up for the photographer. She did well in the orchards and was soon promoted to "straw boss."

The age difference between Sadie and herself was such that Rose was almost a contemporary of her sister's oldest boys. And they took their young, fun-loving aunt to dances in Seattle. It was a good time for Rose—maybe the best in her life. At one of the dances she met Julius Silverman. Eleven years her senior, he was a Russian immigrant, a naturalized citizen who traveled Alaska as a fur buyer for the Hudson's Bay Company.

Although she was almost twenty-eight, Rose's sexual knowledge was limited to her mother's quip that babies "come out where they go in." But Julius was handsome; she was always attracted to a handsome man, and the life he was leading must have seemed romantic to her.

There is a photograph of my mother and father— perhaps it is their wedding picture. He is seated on what appears to be a stanchion on an outside staircase. Rose stands behind him, leaning forward, her arms around his neck, her face lit by a wide, delighted grin. His small smile seems oddly embarrassed.

"He was older—experienced," she would say later. "I thought he would be understanding." But he wasn't, she said. So she adopted the then-not-so-unusual attitude that sex was something a man wanted and a woman endured.

They went to Alaska together. He gave up his adventurous life on the trail, and they became the owners of the North Pole Bakery and Coffee Shop, in Nome. About a year later my sister, Lillian, was born. My mother spoke of that birth in terms of suffering—the near-unbearable pain. She seemed angry that a woman was given this to endure, too. Yet a photograph shows her, still a slim young woman, vivacious and proud, standing beside a wicker carriage with my father, who, in vest and shirtsleeves, has begun to look middle-aged.

The baby was unexpectedly beautiful, with clear blue eyes and black curly hair. And the North Pole Bakery and Coffee Shop was making money—a lot of money. Rose thought about sending for her mother from the Old Country. Maybe marriage wasn't what she had hoped, but, from the beginning, it seems, her desire to enjoy life was stronger than any disappointment and hardship.

She became pregnant again.

Their business had done so well that they decided to cash in, sell the North Pole Bakery and Coffee Shop, and move back to the States, where life was more comfortable. There was a buyer willing to pay $20,000, a fortune in 1928. In what was to be the disastrous turning point in their marriage, Rose left for Seattle, to be joined by my father after he had completed the sale.

This is the story that my mother told: a man named Rotman, who had worked for them in the bakery, made my father a proposition. For a commission, he would take the money from the sale of the bakery and use it to buy furs, which he would then sell for double the price. My father agreed, turned over the money, and never saw Rotman again.

Like many of my mother's memories, this one raises questions. Why would my father agree to such an offer when he, himself, could have bought and sold the furs? And how could Rotman "disappear" in Alaska, which, though geographically huge, was so sparsely populated that anyone's movements were generally known or at least could easily be traced?

Still, I do believe that, somehow, my father had been bilked out of their money. And that, in 1929, Rose found herself penniless, with one small child, pregnant with another, and married to a demoralized and humiliated man. Years later she confessed that many times she had considered leaving him. I am sure this was one of them. But whether from compassion, concern about her children, or something else, she stayed with him. And never threw his terrible mistake in his face.

If it hadn't been that these events coincided with the onset of the Depression, Rose and Julius might have recovered. As it was, it proved to be the beginning of seven harrowing years.

Julius had the idea to go to San Francisco, remembering from his travels a glistening city. I don't know which of the succession of small businesses they tried there first. Perhaps it was the ice-cream parlor. There is a photograph of my father standing behind a plate-glass window, a white apron around his waist, his face grim and strained beneath a sign announcing PEACHES 'N' CREAM FOUNTAIN LUNCH.

There was a delicatessen, a bar and grill, a luncheonette. It was hard work, very hard work, and meant long hours. With each failure we moved from one room in back of a shop to another or, sometimes, to furnished one-room apartments. Creditors hounded my mother and father, and a social worker showed up once, looked at the small dark room in back of the deli, and threatened to take us children away.

It was then that my father began to have pains in his leg. Rose was suspicious. He didn't like to face the creditors. Was this an excuse to hide in the back room?

He went to see a doctor.

"They put him in the hospital," Rose told me years later, "and next thing I know, I get a call from the doctor telling me they got to cut off his leg." Again, my mother's version of what happened is unconvincing.

At the hospital, they injected him with something "experimental," and his leg "turned black" overnight, she said. It was "blood poisoning."

Whatever the cause, his left leg was amputated.

Rose heard him screaming, there in the hospital as she came down the hallway to visit him. Screaming at the pain as they cleansed the wound.

Something went wrong and they had to cut again, removing more of the stump. Afterward, Rose said, they attached weights to his skin to stretch it, so that there would be enough skin to cover the wound. He begged her to remove them.

"I wouldn't blame you for leaving me," he said.

But, of course, she didn't.

Instead, while he was in the hospital, she looked for another business. She found the Model Café, on Polk

Street. Julius could be the cashier, she planned. He could sit on a stool at the end of the long counter. And there was a room behind the kitchen where we could all live.

I don't know how long the Model Café lasted, but afterward came the coffee shop on Franklin Street. And the apartment around the corner on Sutter.

My mother kept trying. She managed to buy an old car and we all went camping in Yosemite.

But my father talked of suicide.

On the day that he took his life, he had been to the doctor and learned that he was to lose his right leg.

FIVE

The Chevy Chase is closed on Sundays and Mother tries to sleep late. She lies on the couch with her back to the room, her head sunk deep in her pillow.

Lillian and I, having finished the comics, pester her to get up and take us someplace. She turns and looks at us, her eyes watery and tired, and says, "You wait, I'm going to get up like a lightning." Then she laughs and turns over.

When she does get up, she takes a long bath, soaking in the tub, wetting the washcloth and spreading it across her chest while she talks. During the week, she's too tired to talk much when she comes home, but on Sundays she tells us stories about the restaurant.

She tells us about a customer named Mr. Solomon, who likes her. He's so short, she says, somebody has to help him climb up on the stool. And one day she turns her back while he's talking to her and when she turns around again, he isn't there. She looks over the counter and there he is on the floor with his feet up in the air. "How could I marry someone like that?" she says with a laugh. "I'd never know where he was."

Then she gets all dressed up in her black princess-style dress with the shiny top and bolero. We watch her put on her rouge and face powder and dab some "Evening in Paris" behind each ear. Then she washes and polishes her rimless eyeglasses and puts them on.

We all go down and get in the old Essex she bought for $25, and Lillian and I climb into the rumble seat and pretend that we're rich kids and Mother is our chauffeur. But the Essex has a way of stalling on Van Ness Avenue, and when that happens, my sister and I scramble out, get behind the car and push, while Mother steers.

One of our favorite places is Golden Gate Park, where we always stop at "Portals of the Past." It's only a pair of columns that before the earthquake used to be the entrance to a beautiful house, Mother explains. But it's still beautiful, because it faces a pond where white swans go gliding by.

We almost always stop at the Japanese Tea Garden, where I like to climb a little, round bridge, so steep that I have to step on wooden strips and pull myself up by the railing to get to the top. And when I'm up there looking down, my knees are wobbly, because the railing is so low there's nothing to hold on to.

Other times we go to Fisherman's Wharf, where Mother buys a bag of prawns fresh from the steaming stone vats on the sidewalk. We sit, three abreast, in the Essex, eating the warm prawns from a paper bag while Mother watches the people passing by and speculates on their personalities and what they do for a living. She ascribes character to physical features. If a person's eyes are close set, he is mean, while small hands on a man imply stinginess. Broad, well-shaped hands indicate the opposite.

Sometimes we go all the way out to the Fun House at Ocean Beach. It's always foggy and cold there, and the ocean is huge and gray and nobody swims in it. Above the Fun House door a life-size Gypsy doll rocks back and forth, holding her sides and laughing. The sound of her laughing in that foggy alleyway gives me the shivers.

But no matter what else we do on Sunday, we end up at the movies. We usually go to the Fox, which is like a palace. That's because it was meant to be an opera house, Mother says. It has a grand curving staircase with golden banisters and scarlet carpeting. In the ladies' room there are small marble dressing tables with mirrors, a stool in the shape of a golden scallop in front of each one.

Sometimes we go to the Golden Gate Theater, where there's a stage show as well as a movie. I remember chorus girls who look as if they're wearing nothing but gold paint, and comedians, like Eddie Foy, Jr., who make my mother laugh, but I don't understand what's funny, and she says I will when I grow up, and Edgar Bergen and Charlie McCarthy ("straight from Hollywood") and Allan Jones singing "The Donkey Serenade" and a big orchestra full of men in tuxedos.

I sit on one side of Mother with Lillian on the other, and I'm eating a U-No Bar and Mother has on her black dress with the satiny top and I can smell her face powder and "Evening in Paris" perfume, and, at that moment, I think she must be the most beautiful woman in the world.

SIX

Maybe she dropped hints that she couldn't go on. That the way we were living couldn't continue. Maybe she even told us what had been going through her mind during those nights when she lay awake on the couch while my sister and I slept in the Murphy bed in that one-room apartment on Sutter Street during the long year and a half after my father died.

That would have been like her. "You can talk to children," she used to say. "You can explain things to them and they'll understand." But if she did speak to us about her fears, about the desperate choice she was considering, I don't remember it.

I do remember how tired she was and how her voice sounded when she came home and looked at the messy room where Lillian and I had spent the afternoon, and how she'd say, "I can't do everything. I can't come home and start cleaning up after you kids after standing on my feet all day. You kids have got to help." And how we would try to remember and try to help.

Once we decided to scrub the kitchen floor. We found a bucket and two bars of laundry soap under the sink. We poured some water on the floor and, in the interest of neatness, stripped down to our underpants. As we were sloshing the soap around, we discovered that, with a little maneuvering, and with our knees pulled up to our chins, we could sit on a bar of soap and, taking turns giving each other a push, slide halfway across the floor. When we tired of that, we experimented with pouring more water on the floor, wedging the laundry bars under our bellies and "swimming" from one end of the kitchen to the other. My mother came home to find us soaked and muddy and half naked and the kitchen a semiflooded disaster.

She never punished us, never hit us or raised her voice. She could laugh in the most hopeless situations. And she was capable of a cold and unbending resolve.

SEVEN

One Sunday in the spring the three of us get all dressed up as usual, but we don't go to Golden Gate Park or Fisherman's Wharf or out to Playland. We're going to a place called Homewood Terrace. It's a long way from Sutter Street to Homewood Terrace on Ocean Avenue, and we take the streetcar, because Mother has sold the old Essex with the rumble seat.

When we get off the streetcar, the place doesn't look anything like Sutter Street. There are no little apartment houses one right next to another. There are a few small stores, but mostly there are walls, walls with houses behind them. At the end of one of the walls there's a sign that says HOMEWOOD TERRACE and a wide driveway leading up a hill.

The three of us walk up the hill. To our right, down a steep embankment covered with ice plants, is a playground where a few children are swinging and running around. Ahead of us is a long, low building set among trees and plants. As we pass, I read the word "Gymnasium" lettered across the front.

Mother is talking to us, saying, "Look at the big playground," and, "Look at all the trees and flowers."

The driveway curves in front of the gymnasium, and up the hillside several two-story white stucco houses come into view. We approach one of them and climb a few steps to the door. Right next to the door is the number 24. When Mother knocks, a lady, with thin silver hair flattened against her scalp in wide marcelled waves, opens it and tells us to come in, as if she were expecting us.

I've never seen such a beautiful room as the one we step into, except in the movies. It is a real living room, with curtains at the windows, big, comfy-looking couches and chairs, a piano, and even a fireplace.

The lady takes us on a tour of the house. She shows us the dining room, with its polished wood floor and four large round tables, and the bedrooms upstairs, with white chenille spreads and filmy white curtains at the windows. I've never been in a house with an upstairs and a down-stairs and real bedrooms.

The lady with the silver hair explains that there aren't many children around today because it's Sunday and their parents have come to take them out for the day. Most of the children have one parent—just like us, she explains to Mother. So on Sundays we have lunch in the kitchen, the lady says, because there are so few of us.

We go down a hallway that skirts the living room and dining room, make a turn, and then there's a door to the kitchen off to the right. It seems to me a very large kitchen, with a high ceiling. A table has been set in the middle of the room, and several children are waiting, standing behind their chairs.

I'm surprised to find that we are going to eat lunch there, too. I'm sure that the silver-haired lady introduces the other children to us, but they are beyond recollection. All that remains of that scene, besides a general sense of the large room, is the memory of an odor, perhaps of cook-ing or disinfectant, or the scent of eucalyptus coming through the open windows, or a combination of all three.

After lunch the lady says wouldn't Mother like to take

us for a walk around the grounds? So the three of us go outside again in our good clothes and Mother asks don't we think the place is nice, like a park? And won't we have fun playing with all the kids?

She bends down and puts her arms around both of us and pulls us close to her, and I breathe in the sweet smell of her face powder and feel the softness of her black satin dress.

That night I wake up in a dark room and hear a clock ticking very loudly and I realize that my mother is gone.

EIGHT

What is there left to laugh about? Rose thought, hearing laughter, hearing two people laughing behind her on the streetcar as she rode, alone, all the way down Market, down where Market got dark under the tall buildings, down past the Chevy Chase—closed now, out of business—all the way down Market to the end, to the Ferry Building. And that night in a coach seat on the train to Seattle, she stayed awake thinking of the terrible thing she had done.

It was May 1938.

From Seattle, Rose caught the First Boat to Nome. She would tell us that she went back to get the money that Rotman owed them, the money he took from Julius all those years earlier. Did she really believe that? Did she really hope that she would find him and somehow retrieve that lost fortune?

Maybe it was easier to dream of that possibility than to admit out loud that she was desperate and almost hopeless except maybe for the hope that Nome would be, as it had been before, a place where a person had a chance. Not like San Francisco, which had been a jinx, she would say later. A city where nothing had gone right, a city of disappointment and despair.

Her roommate on board Alaska Steamship's SS *Baranof* was a young nurse named Johnnie—"a tall drink of water," Mother called her, with a good sense of humor. Both of them were seasick during the long journey. One day it was so rough that Johnnie was thrown out of the top bunk onto the floor, and a vase of flowers someone had given her as a going-away present landed on top of her. She looked so funny, sprawled on the floor, that in spite of my mother's misery, she laughed and so did Johnnie.

Russian Mike was on the jetty when Rose arrived in Nome. Russian Mike from the old days, and he fell on his knees when he saw her, kissing her hands and calling her the beautiful lady with the tiny hands and feet.

There were other people who remembered her, too— remembered the little greenhorn with the Yiddish accent whom Julius Silverman had brought up from Seattle. She was back now, a widow, without him or her children.

Nome had been almost completely destroyed by a fire since Rose had left. And even though it had been rebuilt, it remained little more than a few rows of shacks hugging the edge of the Bering Sea. How did she have the heart, I wonder, to face that bleak and comfortless place? She had to, she would say later.

With her last few dollars, she took a room at Jin Borg's place. The sour-faced little Swede had been a "sporting woman" ten years earlier, but now was respectable, and ran a hotel—a square, two-story building with fresh white paint right on Front Street.

Rose asked all around for work, any kind of work, just to get a start. She would be a cook or a clerk or a waitress. She must have tried every place in Nome—the Nevada Bar and Grill, the North Pole Bakery and Coffee Shop (it was still there—a new building, but the same name), the Northern Commercial Company, Polet's Dry Goods. But there was no work, not even in Nome.

NINE

They called it Homewood Terrace, but its real name was the Pacific Hebrew Orphan Asylum. It had been planned as a model orphanage in those days, the heart of the Depression, meant not necessarily for true orphans but for kids like us, kids with one parent for whom the times were so hard they couldn't take care of their own children. Homewood extended over some thirteen acres on a hill-

side near St. Francis Wood, one of San Francisco's better
residential neighborhoods, out toward the ocean. The
children lived in "cottages," each housing some eighteen
boys and girls and a housemother. We slept in bedrooms,
not dormitories, three or four to a room. Each cottage had
a large living room with a piano and a fireplace, a dining
room, and a small library, separated from the living room
by French doors. The upstairs was divided into boys' and
girls' sides, with the housemother's small bedroom and sitting room in between.

Within Homewood's grounds were a gymnasium, a
playground, a recreation building, which contained a temple and rooms for bible classes, an infirmary, and a nurse
on full-time duty. The property was heavily planted with
shrubs and flowers, and there was a stand of eucalyptus
trees, called "the forest," up the hillside behind the cottages.

The children went to the public schools in the neighborhood, to the movies at the El Rey on Ocean Avenue,
and, occasionally, on outings to special events, such as the
San Francisco World's Fair. There were dances and bas-
ketball games and even plays staged in Homewood's gymnasium.

It would seem that my mother had abandoned us in
Paradise. But, to a child, even Paradise can be terrifying.
I knew that my mother was far away in Alaska. I knew that
she said she would send for us "real soon," but all I really
knew for certain was that my sister and I were alone in
this strange place.

They're not mean to us. Mrs. Gans, the silver-haired lady who is the housemother of Cottage 24, isn't mean to us, but there are so many rules, rules I might break at any minute. And then there would be no one to turn to, no one at all.

You have to eat everything on your plate, you have to scrub the tub after you take a bath, wash out your socks every night, make your bed so there aren't any creases, finish all the chores you're given, stand when a grown-up comes into the room.

I can remember these things, but suppose there are other rules I don't know and so can't remember? What will happen to me?

The kids tell me about punishments. If you rest your elbow on the dining table, an older kid can hit it with a knife handle. If you don't finish your food at mealtimes you have to sit in the dining room until you do, even if you're there all night. The worst punishment is for bed-wetting. One boy had to wear his wet sheet all the next day; another was tied to the toilet for hours.

I am careful, very careful.

I learn not to say much because I never know when I'm going to say something wrong. Like when I'm telling Mrs. Gans how Mother used to take us to Fisherman's Wharf on Sundays and how we would sit in the car and eat hot prawns from a paper bag. Her mouth gets all tight and she looks at me and frowns. Wasn't I supposed to talk about my mother? Is it impolite to eat in a car? Later I discover the reason for her disapproval: Jews aren't supposed to eat shellfish.

I don't know anything about being Jewish. I only know that once, when the teacher was talking about religion at school, I asked my mother what we were. She laughed and said we were Jewish, but what difference did it make?

I sleep in a room with three other girls and I watch what they do. When they get dressed in the morning each one stands near her bed with her back to the others, her bathrobe draped over her shoulders so nobody can see her wriggling into her underwear. So I do that, too.

Libby is the big girl in the room, and the big girls can tell you what to do. She shows me how to make my bed the right way. How to make hospital corners with the sheets and how to fold the bedspread down, so when you pull it up to cover the pillow, there's exactly the right amount. That's the only time Libby talks to me, when she's showing me how to do something.

Once, I wake up in the middle of the night and find myself leaning over a bathtub with a scrub brush in my hand. Libby is standing behind me with her arms folded. "You forgot to wash out the tub," she says.

Sometimes when I'm combing my hair in front of the mirror in the bathroom, Libby stands behind me and says, "I guess you think you're pretty cute, don't you?" And then she tells me to get out of the way.

The older girls choose one of the younger girls to be their special friend. The other big girl in Cottage 24 is

Carol, and Helen Ellis is her special friend. Helen is pretty, with the biggest brown eyes I've ever seen and dark curly hair, and she used to want to be a nun because she was in a convent before Homewood, but now she doesn't know. Carol is pretty, too, and blond, and she's a senior and can do whatever she wants.

I'd like to be an older girl's friend, but there is only Libby, and she doesn't ask me.

Helen gets to be in the room with Carol and Libby when they are wrapping the pads. That's this thing that they do all the time, and it's a secret and nobody else is allowed in the room when they're doing it. But we stand in the doorway and watch.

First, they tear up the newspaper into single pages and they spread these across the top of one of the beds. Then they open a box full of big white gauzy pads, like giant Band-Aids, and they lay one of these on each piece of newspaper. All the time they're doing this, they're laughing and giggling and telling each other stories in low voices so we can't hear. They wrap up each pad in newspaper, folding over the ends, so you can't see it at all, and then stack them all up.

I know that the pads are for what happens to girls when they get older, and I know that they wrap them up because it's embarrassing and you're not supposed to let anybody, especially boys, see the pads. I also know that it'll happen to me, too, when I'm bigger and then I'll get to be in the bedroom wrapping the pads, too.

But, now, I have to stand in the doorway, because I'm not an older girl's special friend.

Meanwhile, I strive to be a model orphan. I do all my chores with a thoroughness that brings compliments from the housemother and even from Dr. Langer, the director of Homewood. I do chores I don't even have to do. I'm quiet, do well in school, am extremely polite. And, most of the time, I'm afraid.

Only when I'm alone do I feel safe. There's a small bathroom downstairs in Cottage 24, under the stairs. It has only one stall and I can lock the door. I go there whenever I can, whenever I won't be missed, and I hide in that stall, feeling that no one knows where I am, that no one can find me. And I discover hiding spots among the plants outdoors. I crawl between the tall hydrangea bushes and find a piece of clear ground just big enough so that if I scrunch down, knees under my chin, I'm completely hidden.

TEN

The funny feeling in my chest happens in the afternoons. At least, that's when I notice it. It's after we've been in the playground. That's what we do after lunch, after the chores are done—we go to the playground.

What I do there is lie down in the border of weeds at the edge of the playground. I lie on my back looking up, so all I see are the tops of the weeds and the sky. When I squint, the weeds go all blurry and I pretend I'm somewhere in a meadow and that these are wildflowers all around me. I can hear the other kids yelling and running about nearby, but it doesn't bother me. I still can pretend I'm far away in a meadow.

But when it gets late in the afternoon, the fog starts rolling in. All of a sudden, the sun disappears, and it's chilly and damp and all the color is gone from the weeds. And then the bell rings and it's time to go back to the cottages.

The kids head for the stairs at the end of the playground, and it is when I look back at the empty swings and seesaws and the sand all ruffled up with footprints and the fog hanging lower and lower that I notice this feeling in my chest. It doesn't hurt, really, it's more like an ache or a hollow, like a hole in the middle of my chest.

I walk up the hill toward Cottage 24, up the narrow cement pathway between the bushes, which are just dark and scary shapes on either side of me. The lights are on in Cottage 24, in the dining room where I'll be sitting down pretty soon with all the other kids, and there'll be this funny smell that I always notice when I come back to the cottage—not a bad smell but a different one, not like anyplace else I ever lived—and I'll sit at the table and have to eat everything on my plate, even though I'm not hungry because of this funny achy feeling in my chest, and I'll wonder if I'm sick, I'll wonder if I have something real bad, and maybe I'll even die. But I won't say anything about it. How can I say that there's a hole in my chest?

ELEVEN

Mrs. Gans asks, "What's the matter with you?"

I'm sitting at the table staring at the lima beans on my plate and I can't eat them. But if I don't, I'll be punished, like Jerry Katz.

He hates liver, and we have it once a week. Then Jerry has to stay in the dining room all by himself after everybody else is in the living room playing Monopoly or listening to the radio. He sits there all alone with all the empty chairs around him, cutting the liver into tinier and tinier pieces. He spears one tiny little piece at a time on his fork and then sticks it inside his lower lip and just holds it there. Sometimes Jerry is still there, sitting all alone at a big table in the dining room, when everyone else goes to bed.

But instead of making me stay at the table, Mrs. Gans says I look sick and I have to go to the infirmary. Right now.

The infirmary is next door to Cottage 24, connected by a cement path. It's dark out, and behind me I can hear the kids talking in the dining room and the dishes and silverware clattering. Up ahead of me, the infirmary is dark except for a light in one of the upstairs windows.

The front door is unlocked and I walk into a little lobby that smells of iodine. A light goes on over my head and the nurse comes down the stairs. She's wearing a stiff white uniform. "Well, what's the matter with you?" she says.

I don't know what's the matter with me. I don't remember the hole in my chest; I just remember that Mrs. Gans said I looked sick. The nurse is staring at me like she doesn't think I'm really sick. I think I should go back to Cottage 24.

But she says, "Okay, come on upstairs."

On the second floor there's a room with two lines of beds, four on each side. They're all made up with white sheets tucked in very tight. The walls are bare and white, and there's one big light on the ceiling in the middle of the room.

The nurse tells me to get undressed and get into bed. I look at all those empty beds and wish I was back at Number 24, but I take off my dress and climb into one of the beds in my underpants and shirt. The sheets feel cold against my skin. Then the nurse sticks a thermometer under my tongue and leaves the room.

I lie there looking up at the ceiling, the sharp point of the thermometer cutting into that stretchy part under my tongue, the sheets so tight I feel like I'm strapped down, and I wonder what the punishment is for pretending to be sick. The nurse comes back and pulls the thermometer out of my mouth. She holds it up above her head and looks at it, but she doesn't tell me what it says. She turns out the light and walks out of the room.

Even in the dark I can see the empty white beds glowing all around me. What is she going to do to me if I'm not sick? Maybe she's going to send me someplace else, someplace they send kids who pretend to be sick.

In the morning the nurse comes and sticks a thermometer in my mouth again. I pray that it's 104. She holds it up to the light, shakes it, then just stands by the bed with her hands on her hips, looking at me. Finally she says, "Well, you know what I think, miss? I think you're a faker. You better just get your clothes on and get out of here."

My face is red-hot. I get dressed and run down the stairs. I don't want to go back to Cottage 24. I don't want to go anyplace. Outside, I crawl between the hydrangea bushes and hide.

I'm sitting there under the bushes for so long I'm getting cold. But I have figured something out: I've figured out that it's not a good idea to get sick or to go to the infirmary. Even if Mrs. Gans tells me I look sick, and even if I'm sure, really sure, that there's a hole in my chest and I'm going to die, I won't go to the infirmary. I'll just die, and then the nurse will have to take back what she said—she'll have to take back that I'm a faker.

TWELVE

They've cut my sister's hair. But she isn't upset; she doesn't even mention it.

Lillian is in Cottage 24, too. She doesn't sleep in the same room as I do, but I see her every day. I'm glad my sister is here. That is, I would be if I thought about it. But, of course, I don't. Why would I? She's always been there.

Mrs. Gans and Dr. Langer, the director, always call us "the Silverman girls," as if we were the same person. I don't mind. Because usually they're saying, "The Silverman girls are no trouble." We're quiet, do our chores, and never try to run away like Marvin, "the Snake," does, escaping only a few blocks down Ocean Avenue before Dr. Langer in his old black car catches up with him. And we never snip off all the tufts on our chenille bedspreads, as Ada Fleischman did.

We don't talk about the way it was before, Lillian and I, or about Mother, or about when Mother is going to send for us and when we'll be going to Alaska. Or about anything else. As far as I can tell, my sister doesn't talk to anyone. And it seems like nothing matters to her—even that they cut off her hair. It's thick and kinky, my sister's hair, and Mother used to braid it sometimes or else pull it back away from her face with an elastic ribbon and it looked pretty. But now it's short and sticks out in two dark triangles behind her ears.

And it doesn't matter to her that Henry Richmond and Joe Tarver, the big boys in Cottage 24, call her "duck," because they say she waddles. Lillian doesn't even seem to hear them. It's as if she isn't there. That's how it seems to me now, in memory, that my sister wasn't really there. Because if she had been, she would remember some of the things that happened to her while we were in Homewood—which she doesn't. Not even the time she spilled the milk.

It occurs one day when we're all having lunch in the dining room—it's Saturday, so there are tablecloths, and Lillian, like the rest of us, is dressed up, wearing the maroon taffeta dirndl dress that Mother had bought her, the one she used to wear on Sundays when we all went out to Golden Gate Park—she's wearing that taffeta dirndl dress with patent-leather shoes, and she's carrying four pitchers of milk into the dining room. That's her job, to help serve the meals.

She's carrying the pitchers by their handles, two in each hand, as she always does, but this time she slips in the middle of the dining room, right in the middle, among the four tables. She lands on her rear end, sits with her legs spread out and milk dripping from her hair and down over her glasses and onto her taffeta dress.

And everybody is laughing at her. Everybody except me. Laughing at my sister sitting on the floor, with the milk dripping all over her, dripping off her thick hair and down the beautiful taffeta dress that Mother had bought for her. But Lillian isn't crying, she isn't even red in the face. She just looks as if she doesn't know what happened.

These are my memories then, of my sister absent,

really—not connecting with anyone or anything. And yet, two things make me wonder if my memory lies. One is the photograph—the only photograph of the two of us from that time in Homewood. In the picture, Lillian and I are standing close together, she is caught in the midst of a gesture, she's almost smiling. Her arm is around my shoulder, as if that is where it would naturally be, and I am half turned toward her, almost huddled against her, looking out at the camera from the protective circle of my sister's arm.

The other thing that makes me question my memory of my sister's "absence" is the way she behaves with the little girl, Dorothy. I say "little" because Dorothy seems younger than I, although, as I recall, there were no children younger than I at Homewood. Dorothy doesn't live with us in Cottage 24. And the only time we are with her is on Sundays. That's when most of the kids' parents, their one parent, that is, come to take them out for the afternoon. Only Lillian and I and Dorothy and a few other kids are left at Homewood, kids whose parents are too far away to take them out. Like Freddie, who Mrs. Gans says is a refugee, which means he's German and he doesn't even have a mother or a father, or maybe he does, but nobody knows where they are. Nobody likes Freddie. He gets angry and flushed when he doesn't want to eat something—peanut butter, for instance. But he doesn't have to eat it and he doesn't get punished, either, and that's because he's a "refugee" and his parents are further away than anybody else's, if he has any.

Those of us left on Sunday sit together on the gym steps overlooking the empty playground. And the little girl named Dorothy sits with us there every Sunday. I don't even know what cottage she lives in, but she always wears this dark blue coat with a beautiful dark blue velvet collar. She must have had it from before she was in Homewood, because nobody there has a coat with a velvet collar. Dorothy wears the coat, even though it has worn spots and her arms stick out below the sleeves, because it is from before.

Anyway, on Sunday afternoons we all just sit up there on the gym steps looking out over the empty playground and beyond Homewood's walls to the red tile rooftops. We look at these houses where other kids live and maybe go out in a car with their mother or father and sisters and brothers and we look out toward the beach, where the Fun House is with the Gypsy lady laughing and laughing all by herself in a glass cage above the entrance. And out beyond that is the ocean.

You can't see the ocean from Homewood, but you know it's out there, because that's where the fog comes from. Rolling in every afternoon, a heavy round curl of fog, stretching from one end of the sky to the other. When it unfolds above you, it turns everything beneath it dark and cold.

And when that happens, little Dorothy starts to cry, crying, it seems, because of the fog. She cries and cries until my sister, who doesn't even appear to be paying attention, slides over next to her, pulls her close, and holds her, until the little girl stops crying.

THIRTEEN

Rose did the rounds of Front Street every day, she told us later. Checking all the stores, asking people if anything had come up, if they'd heard of anything. Like everyone else in town, the owner of the Nome Liquor Store knew that Rose Silverman was looking for work. Cappy Green didn't know my mother from the old days. He'd been living in Candle then, an Eskimo village about 140 miles northeast of Nome, running a trading post with his father. But Cappy was friendly. Partly, it was just the normal small-town friendliness. Partly, maybe, it was because she was Jewish, like him, and there weren't many Jews in Nome. Partly, perhaps, because she was a woman all alone.

At any rate, when Rose stopped by his store on her rounds one day, Cappy told her that Hank Graff had been in mentioning that he needed a cook for his gold-mining operation. If she was interested, Cappy said, she could find Graff at the Nevada.

She ran right over. Sure enough, Graff's cook hadn't showed up on the First Boat like she was supposed to, the mining season had already started and he needed someone right away. Rose told Graff that she could cook, and he told her that she had the job. It paid five dollars a day, plus room and board.

The camp was up in the Kougarok, a gold-mining area skirting the river for which it was named, in the middle of the Seward Peninsula, more than 100 miles north of

Nome. The Kougarok was a roadless wilderness with no settlements other than a handful of gold-mining camps, most of which were serviced by bush pilots from Nome.

Graff's outfit consisted of a cookhouse, a bunkhouse, a couple of sheds, and the gold-mining pit. There were no other camps for miles around. Rose was the only woman among some ten miners. She had a small, bare room at one end of the cookhouse, and she prepared six meals a day, feeding a day crew and a night crew. She did not only all the cooking but also the baking—a skill she had never needed and therefore had never acquired. Her first tries at baking bread resulted in a lot of kidding from the men. "Hey, Rose," they'd say, hoisting a loaf, "bring me over one of them hacksaws."

They made fun of her Yiddish accent, too, mimicking the way she interchanged *v* and *w* so that "vegetable" became "wegetable." She didn't mind. She'd always been able to laugh at herself and didn't take offense.

"What accent?" she'd say, "I don't hear nothing."

Graff liked her, and when he thought his men were ribbing her too much, would tell them to shut up. "Rose is smarter than all you roughnecks put together," he'd tell them.

Every week during the cleanup, when they removed the gold from the sluice boxes, Graff would tell Rose to pick out something for herself. And each time she would select a tiny nugget, so that by the end of the season she would have a small vial full. (The delicate bracelet she eventually had made from these and other nuggets she collected over the years is one of the few mementos that I have of my mother.) If any romance developed, I never heard about it. But, from the story of the nuggets, it sounds as if Hank Graff might have been "sweet" on her, as she would say.

Rose worked hard, but the job seemed easy compared to the long hours and the terrible responsibilities of her days in San Francisco. She didn't talk about us, about the children she had left behind. Not to Graff, not to anybody. What would have been the use, she said later. None of them would understand what a mother goes through. She wrote to us once a week. The letters had to wait for the bush pilot's intermittent pick-ups, so they arrived two or three at a time.

We wrote her, too. And when our letters came, she took them to her room, where nobody would see her crying. "I just wanted to know you were all right," she'd say afterward. "I had nightmares about them hurting you. I'd wake up shaking and sick to my stomach."

I believe her. I believe she was anguished. But, later— listening to her memories of those days, her descriptions of how she had time in the afternoons to take long walks alone on the tundra, how she enjoyed picking wildflowers and, later in the season, gathering blueberries, which grew on ground-hugging bushes, how she read in the quiet of the cookhouse while the day crew worked in the pit and the night crew slept in the bunkhouse—I came to believe that these days were a respite for her.

At last, she had some peace.

FOURTEEN

The letters come in small envelopes edged with red, white, and blue stripes. "My dearest babies," they say. She tells us that she has a job, a good job in a gold-mining camp. She tells us that it pays her five dollars a day, and that's good money. And she can keep all of it because she has a place to stay, too, and all her meals, so she'll be able to send for us real soon.

Be good, my babies, she writes—don't worry, don't be sad, my babies, I'm doing the best I can, we'll all be together soon.

When I hold the pieces of lined white paper in my hand and see my mother's small, careful handwriting, I can smell her face powder and feel her softness. *"Kleine maideleh,"* she calls me, pressing my face against her breast, *"kleine maideleh."*

I tell Elaine Krasnow, who's my new friend and who stutters and wears union suits because she's from Chicago—I tell her that I am going to Alaska. And she asks, "Where's that?" And I don't know. Except it's far away.

But weeks and months go by, and after a while it's hard to remember what my mother looks like and when I try to remember, all I can see are her words in pencil on the lined white paper.

FIFTEEN

Everybody has a job in Cottage 24. The big girls fix the meals and the big boys polish the furniture, scrub and wax the floors, and keep the kitchen clean. The younger kids help them out. Lillian serves meals; my job is drying dishes. What I find out is, I like to work. I like wiping the dishes and making them shine. I like drying the dishes fast, showing that I can keep up with Henry Richmond, the big boy who washes them.

Henry's a senior in high school, and he's tall and chunky and has a lot of sand-colored curly hair and wears funny round glasses and has been in Homewood for as long as he can remember. He straps thick rubber pads around his legs because he says he has "water on the knees" from scrubbing the kitchen floor every day of his life.

When I'm finished drying the dishes, I do other things— things I don't even have to do. Like wiping off the base-boards, which is really Henry's job, and climbing up on the counter and cleaning the glass on the cabinet doors. I rub them with balled-up newspaper and make them really shiny.

When Mrs. Gans comes by and sees me cleaning and scrubbing, she pats my head and says, "All my kids should be like you."

Henry likes to play jokes on people. Like when I was standing at the sink scrubbing the burner covers from the stove, he watched me for a while and then told me I should run down to the supply room in the administration building and get a can of elbow grease. I was on my way out to get it before he told me he was just kidding. And then he says things like, "How did I ever get along without you?"

When I'm working in the kitchen with Henry, everything seems all right. Even though Eddie Parker is there, too. Eddie is just about one year older than I. He's skinny, and his lanky hair hangs down over one eye. He's always squinting and blinking real fast and jerking his head from side to side and rubbing his fists together one on top of the other.

When he passes me in the hallway behind the kitchen and nobody else is around, he presses his hand against me, right between my legs, and says, "I like to feel your fuck." I'm pretty sure that's dirty, but I don't say anything.

SIXTEEN

Henry likes to play jokes on Eddie Parker. One day Henry makes a little hole in an egg with a needle. Then he sucks out all the insides and puts the empty eggshell back in a carton in the pantry. When Eddie comes in to put the dishes away, Henry drops his arm around Eddie's shoulders and says he's going to let Eddie help him with a magic trick. Eddie looks up at Henry and his eyes are blinking really fast and he starts rolling his fists on top of each other and he says he doesn't want to, in this whiny voice.

But Henry pretends he doesn't hear Eddie. He just smiles and walks over to the pantry and shows Eddie the carton of eggs. "I'm going to break one of these eggs on your head," he tells Eddie, "but because of my magical powers, absolutely nothing will happen."

Eddie tries to run away, but Henry, who's ten times bigger than he is, just grabs him by his skinny arm and pulls him back and tells him he is lucky to be part of this magic demonstration.

"You have to trust me, Eddie," Henry says, speaking gently, softly. "If you don't trust me, the trick won't work."

Eddie keeps trying to twist away, but Henry's squeezing his arm and he can't get loose. He's blinking so fast you can't see his eyelids.

Very slowly, Henry reaches in and pulls out the empty egg and holds it over Eddie's head for a while, saying some words that sound like a foreign language. Then he smashes the egg on top of Eddie's head, grinding the shells into his hair. Eddie screams.

Mrs. Gans comes rushing in through the swinging doors to the dining room, patting her hair and looking all worried and asking, "What are you up to now, Henry?"

But Henry just smiles. He points to Eddie's hair. There's no goo at all, only a few pieces of eggshell. "A little magic, Mrs. Gans," he says.

She looks up at Henry, who is much bigger than she is, waves her hands at the ceiling, and totters away.

SEVENTEEN

When the ground froze, Graff's camp shut down for the season. Most of the men would be catching the Last Boat from Nome, taking their season's payoff to families waiting for them Outside or maybe just to the bars along Seattle's waterfront. Rose, on the other hand, was facing the winter in Nome. But she had her season's wages, too, and with them she could get a place to stay and look around for "an opportunity."

She rented a cabin. A shack, really. So cold that when she mopped the kitchen, the water froze on the floor. She slept with her clothes on and everything else she owned piled on top of her.

Again she looked for work, the wind blowing so hard that she could make her way only by clinging to the buildings along Front Street. There was nothing. Nothing, that is, except cleaning house for the few well-off women whose husbands worked for the Company—the United States Smelting, Refining and Mining Company, whose three gold dredges were the biggest operation in Nome, or for Lomen Brothers, the lighterage firm that owned the tugs and barges that unloaded the ships and—as everybody complained—charged as much to get goods from the boat to the jetty as it cost to bring them all the way from Seattle. So Rose became a house cleaner. She would take any work she could get. But it never made her humble.

Years later, her voice trembling with anger, she would tell me of how a Nome matron, showing her out as some guests arrived, found her back door frozen shut. She couldn't get it open, no matter how hard she tried. "She yanked and yanked, and got all red in the face," Rose recalled. "She'd rather kill herself than let me walk through the front door. But she couldn't get that back door open and she had to let 'the maid' walk through the living room in front of her guests," Rose remembered bitterly.

How my mother's spirit survived during that first winter, I have no idea. What schemes, what desperate contingencies, went through her mind as she lay shivering under piles of clothing in that freezing cabin?

She wrote us faithfully, her letters always cheerful, always promising to send for us as soon as she could. There was no further mention—ever—of Rotman or of her plan to recover the long-lost fortune.

EIGHTEEN

We are sitting together, all of us girls from Cottage 24, sitting on the soft flowered couches and chairs in the living room. Even the big girls, all of us together, and there's a large basket of socks in the middle of the floor.

Some of us have darning knobs, they're smooth and made of wood and have a handle you can hold onto. But I just have a lightbulb because there aren't enough knobs to go around. But it doesn't matter. I like to darn. The darning needle is big and the yarn is thick. Because it is so thick, you have to thread it a special way: you fold it over and force it up against the hole in the needle, pushing the wool until you can catch a piece of it on the other side and pull it through.

I make a good weave, neat and tight. I space the yarn evenly, threading it back and forth across the hole, making a grid of wool, then working the needle over and under, over and under, pulling the yarn over and under the lattice I've made. Using the tip of the big needle, I press each line of yarn up against the last one, pushing it tight so there are no spaces.

It's light and sunny in the living room of Number 24, and *One Man's Family* is playing on the radio, on the big radio against the wall, and the window is open and the smell of flowers and eucalyptus is blowing in with the curtains and the older girls are laughing and talking and I am nestled into the couch and I am making a very good darn.

NINETEEN

On Saturday morning, all the kids from all the cottages go to the Temple. It's very still in the Temple, the walls are thick and hold in the silence. The light through the stained-glass window turns blue and spatters across the stucco of the opposite wall. Beneath me, through the thin cotton of my dress, I can feel the polished, slippery wood of the bench as my rear end slides into the depression between the seat and the back.

Mr. Werner, the music teacher, sits at the organ, and his broad back stretches the tweed jacket he always wears. When he is teaching us the songs during singing practice every Saturday afternoon, he gets mad and yells and his neck turns red and his hair falls in his face. But now he is just sitting at the organ waiting for Dr. Langer to tell him when to play.

The organ thunders all the way up to the ceiling and I sing as loud as I can—"Oh, Worship the King"—and I can see a king in a golden carriage decorated with curlicues and pulled by prancing horses. And when we sing "Out of the Depths, Oh Lord, I Cry to Thee," the words seem like my very own: "Out of the depths, Oh Lord, I cry to Thee;/Oh hear my voice this day,/And let Thine ear to me attentive be,/Almighty, when I pray." I see myself standing in a deep hole, the kind that Tarzan or Jungle Jim falls into when the bad guys set a trap for them. And I am crying out, yelling straight up, out of the hole. And, way above me, way up in the sky, God is there, even though I can't see Him. And I just need to get His attention, so I sing loud and in tune, just the way Mr. Werner taught us, and then I know God hears me. The chords Mr. Werner plays on the organ bounce off the walls, jumping back and forth, so it's as if I hear them from all sides and they fill up the whole Temple and I feel full of them, too.

We sing the responses in Hebrew, and I don't know what they mean—I just sound out the words—but they are mysterious and magical, like an incantation.

Dr. Langer, who's a rabbi, stands up on this platform and talks to us. He's small and thin and wears dark suits that make him look smaller and thinner. He must never eat, he's so holy. His eyes are large and brown and seem always to be looking just above us, at something else.

He speaks in a soft voice and tells us stories from the Bible like about how Moses led his people into the wilderness to escape Pharaoh. And how the sons of Israel had promised Joseph that they would carry his bones out of Egypt when they went to the Promised Land. "How would it have been if Moses had 'forgotten' to bring Joseph's bones from the wilderness," Dr. Langer says, "like some of you 'forget' to change your bedsheets every Monday even though they smell to high heaven?" And his large eyes grow very sad.

That makes me sad, too, and, even though I always change my bedsheets on Mondays and do everything I'm told, I promise myself I will never forget and I will work harder.

Behind Dr. Langer, up on the platform where he stands, is a small box whose opening is covered with dark red velvet curtains. On special occasions, like the High Holy Days and when a boy is bar mitzvahed, he turns to face the box and pulls open the curtains and reaches in for this big double scroll. Dr. Langer lifts it out gently and then

cradles it against his shoulder as if it were a baby. It is the
Torah, and I don't know what that is, except that it is holy
and precious.

At the end of the service, Dr. Langer always says, "May
the Lord bless you, may the Lord make His face to shine
upon you," and when we walk outside the sun *is* shining
on us and right there in a cement triangle is a bed of California poppies. Before they bloom, each poppy wears a
little green pointed hood. I look for the poppies whose
hoods are turning brown and beginning to separate, and
then I pull them off and watch the golden petals fall loose.
When I stroke them, they feel like satin.

The kids stand around outside the Temple before going
back to the cottages, the big boys and girls laughing and
talking together, all dressed up in their best clothes—the
boys wear suits and the girls flowery dresses. Carol, the
big girl from Cottage 24, has on yellow silk stockings one
day, and Eddie Parker stares at them and then puts his
hand over his mouth and tells me that it looks like Carol
had an accident.

Then we go back to Cottage 24 for a special Sabbath
lunch. The white tablecloths are on the tables and I can
smell the roast lamb with little slivers of garlic stuck
under the skin, which I helped fix that morning, my fingers still smelling like garlic, and everybody is in their
dress-up clothes.

And sometimes, later on Saturday afternoon, after
we've changed clothes and had singing practice, we'll go,
all together, down the wide bumpy pavement of the drive-

way, out between the big square gateposts, out onto
Ocean Avenue to the El Rey Theater, where they let us in
without our having to pay anything, all of us together. And
there are two movies and once, I remember, the second
one was W. C. Fields in *My Little Chickadee,* but we had
to leave before it was over, we always have to leave when
one of the big boys tells us, comes whispering in the dark
to tell us it's time. That's the rule, because then it's time
to leave, no matter what.

And at night, every night, I say this prayer:

Under the shadow of Thy wing, O Lord,
I lay me down to sleep;
No fear have I, for well I know a loving watch shall keep.
Through all the days and all the years, whatever
    may befall,
God make me honest, kind, truthful and loving unto all.
Shema Yisraeil: Adonai Eloheinu, Adonai Echad.
Hear O Israel, the Lord our God, the Lord is One.

Once I've said it, I can go to sleep.

TWENTY

When school starts, Mrs. Gans sends me to Mrs. Kerpil's
room in the basement of the Temple building to get new
clothes. Mrs. Kerpil wears a hairnet, and her eyes bulge

out like a frog's. I stand across a counter from her and she reaches into one of the cardboard cartons that are open all around her, pulls out a dress, leans across the counter, holds it up against me and says, "That'll fit."

Mrs. Kerpil also gives me a coat with a belt and a big fur collar that covers up half my face. It looks like somebody's grandmother's coat. I hate it, but I'm afraid to hide it like Ada Fleischman did with the pink-and-green dress Mrs. Kerpil gave her that Ada said would make her puke if she had to wear it. She rolled it up in a ball and hid it in the locker room at Cottage 24, behind the shoe-shining stuff.

The coat is bad, but the underpants are worse. They're too big. Mrs. Kerpil says I'll grow into them, but every time I wear them I'm afraid they're going to fall down. And one time they even do, but nobody's looking, so I just pull them back up. When I'm walking to school with the other kids I have to kind of stick my hand between the buttons of my coat and hold on to my underpants through my dress so they won't fall down around my ankles.

We grammar school kids go to Admiral Farragut, which is a few blocks from Homewood. And we all walk together down the steep driveway and out between the posts onto the regular streets, where the air smells different—damper and fresher. When I get bigger, I'll go to Aptos Junior High School, where red and orange nasturtiums spill over a white stucco wall and onto the sidewalk.

Sometimes the regular kids, the ones who live in the ritzy neighborhood outside Homewood, run by us and yell

"Dirty Kikes." And Jerry Katz got into a fight with one of them. But, to me, they seem like shadows in the fog. I'm just trying to keep my underpants from falling down.

TWENTY-ONE

I have to have my tonsils out. I don't know why. I don't have a sore throat or anything.

Some of the other kids have had their tonsils out. They tell me your throat really hurts afterward, but that you get to have ice cream, even if it's early in the morning.

Dr. Langer drives me to the hospital. Just him and me, all by ourselves, in a car. I sit in the front seat next to him, and he's wearing his dark suit and hat.

At the hospital, a nurse takes me away to a children's ward, a long room lined with beds separated by glass partitions. The nurse smiles a lot and is big and strong, and she lifts me up onto the bed and takes my clothes off, as if I am too sick to do it myself.

"There you are, all high and dry," she says.

And I think she means that the bed is very high and the floor a long way below me.

Right next to me, through the glass partition, there is a boy who looks like he is my age. His parents are standing by his bed, bending over him. They seem young to be somebody's parents. They look across at me and smile, and when the nurse goes by, they stop her and ask her something, and I think it is about me, because then the three of them turn to look at me.

I just lie there for a long time with nothing to do. I can hear a kid crying somewhere down the ward, but it seems pretty far away. Maybe they forgot about me, I think—maybe I won't have to have my tonsils out.

After a while, the mother of the boy next to me comes around to my side of the partition and stands by my bed. She is pretty and slender. "We'd like to buy you a present," she says. "Would you rather have a handkerchief or some perfume?"

I say "perfume" right away.

Later they come back with a big bottle of "Tweed" that has a spray and everything. It is the first time I've ever had perfume.

Having your tonsils out is not that bad.

But then the big nurse who had undressed me and some other nurses come and lift me onto a rolling table and wheel me down a corridor. The big nurse touches my hair and says, "Such pretty curls." I watch the lights go by overhead: blink, white ceiling, blink, white ceiling, blink. And I know I am never coming back.

I am in the operating room. I see shiny machines against the walls. Somebody puts something over my nose and mouth and tells me to breathe and count backward from 100. I say "A hundred," take a deep breath, and suffocate. When I wake up the next morning my throat only feels a little sore, and nobody gives me ice cream.

Dr. Langer comes to pick me up. I feel special that he is driving me, all by myself, in the car.

As we near Homewood, we pass the El Rey. "Do you want to see a movie?" Dr. Langer asks me.

Something like a spark jumps inside my chest. I forget about the hospital and about my sore throat. Dr. Langer is going to take me, just me, to the movies.

"Yes," I say.

"Well, there it is," he says, pointing to the El Rey as we drive by.

Then I understand it is a joke.

TWENTY-TWO

Sometime during that winter, that first hard winter in Nome, Cappy Green asked Rose if she would cook for him and his father. Cappy had a wife, and a family, too, but they were in Seattle. In Nome, he lived alone in rooms at the back of his store. For much of the year, he was a bachelor. Cappy and his father took their meals there, although the old man, a widower, had a rather large house on the street behind the Federal Building. Rose was to help out in the store, too. I don't know what financial arrangement Cappy offered. Whatever it was, it looked better than cleaning houses for an hourly wage, and she accepted.

Rose was a good cook. She served plain but tasty meals. But the old man was fussy and "a pain in the neck." Everything had to be just so. Portions of canned string beans must be counted out, exactly the same number for each of them. The same with the canned cherries and anything else she might serve. Rose despised pettiness.

But Cappy wasn't like that. He was "easygoing" and treated her with respect. And, probably, more than that. For he began taking her to movies at the Dream Theatre and to dances held at the school gym.

In a photograph from that time, a group portrait taken at a costume party, Mother stands next to Cappy at the far end of the last row. They're not in costume. Rose wears a demure dark dress, Cappy's in a suit. It's a blurry picture, but still I can recognize them. And I see a smile on my mother's face and I see her small hand resting familiarly in the crook of Cappy's arm.

Maybe things started looking better to Rose. Maybe she had a dream about her mother. When she dreamed of her mother, she told me years later, that meant good luck. A dream of a baby foretold misfortune.

TWENTY-THREE

We are lucky to have Mrs. Gans as our housemother. That's what the kids from the other cottages say. She isn't mean and bossy like the housemother next door, in Number 26. I can see Mrs. Levy from the window of my bedroom upstairs, sitting on a stool on the cement path outside the kitchen window of Number 26. She is so fat that her rear end spills over the seat of the stool, but she has a very small head and her hair is pulled back tight, so her head looks even smaller. She sits outside, yelling orders through the kitchen window to the kids working inside.

Mrs. Gans hardly ever gets mad or yells at us. She says she is tired of raising kids. She has a grown-up one of her own. I know his name is Julian, but I have never seen him or even a picture of him. Maybe she has one in her rooms upstairs, but nobody is ever allowed to go in there. It's private.

I sit at Mrs. Gans's table in the dining room now, right next to her, like I am special, like I am her favorite, ever since I came back from the infirmary. And on Friday evenings I watch her light the candles.

On Fridays, there are white tablecloths in the dining room of Cottage 24. And two tall white candles on the table in front of Mrs. Gans. She wears her silky, navy blue dress with the little pink and white flowers all over, and the flat waves in her hair are covered with a wispy silver hairnet. When she leans forward over the candles I watch the golden light from the flames play over her face—her soft, wrinkled face—as she recites a prayer in Hebrew.

Afterward, in the living room, Mrs. Gans lets me sit on the floor next to her chair, where she is crocheting and listening to the radio. "Are you worried about Cappy?" she asks me one evening after we had a letter from Mother. Mrs. Gans reads our letters before we even get them. I think maybe Dr. Langer does, too. Or someone else in his office. That's the way it is at Homewood. "Are you worried that your mother might be thinking about getting married?"

My mother writes about Cappy, the man she is working for. He is nice to her, she says. But her letters seem like stories in a book. Stories about people in a faraway place. What do they have to do with me or with Cottage 24 or Mrs. Gans?

It's not that I can't remember my mother, or what it was like before. I could remember, if I wanted to—remember the apartment on Sutter Street and Lillian and me by ourselves, waiting for Mama. Remember Sundays and Mother's black dress with the bolero, and sitting next to her in the movies, and the three of us crowded together in the front seat of the Essex. And, if I tried, I could even remember the smell of "Evening in Paris" and the rose-petal smell of her face powder.

But I don't think about any of it because, when I do, my chest aches and I can't eat what's on my plate. Besides, none of it seems real like Cottage 24 does, like the library with the French doors and the sunny window seat, a window seat like I've seen in the movies, where I sit now and read books—thick, worn books with threads hanging out of the covers because of all the kids who have read them—sitting in the window seat reading *The Red Fairy Book,* and then *The Blue Fairy Book,* and even *The Green Fairy Book,* and all the dog books I can find by Albert Payson Terhune, like *The Heart of a Dog.*

And every week, there in the library, I sit around the heavy wooden table with the other girls of Cottage 24 and the volunteer ladies who teach us how to knit and crochet, and I have my own knitting needles and yarn and I am knitting a scarf, a real scarf. And the volunteer lady puts her hands under mine to show me how to make a loop and stick the needle through it and throw the yarn the right way.

And in the evenings after dinner sometimes all of us kids lie spread out on the soft rug of the living-room floor and play Chinese checkers or Monopoly, and listen to the radio. And sometimes funny things happen, like when Henry Richmond started sniffing and looking around the room and then said, "Somebody laid a bomb," and looked at Eddie Parker and said, "Don't you have to go to the bathroom, Eddie?" and Eddie squinted and blinked and shook his head, but Henry grabbed him by the back of his shirt, anyway, and said, "Oh, I think you do," and dragged him across the living-room rug toward the bathroom.

Other times, Werner, one of the German refugee kids,

except he's not really a kid, but almost eighteen, sits at the piano with his back toward everybody and plays beautiful music, and everybody is quiet then and listens.

At these times, I don't remember Mother and the way it was before, and I don't feel the hollow ache in my chest.

TWENTY-FOUR

It is summertime and we roller-skate outdoors after dinner. We skate along the broad driveway that circles Homewood's grounds. All of us—the big boys and big girls, too—skating past the embankment of ice plants that falls away to the playground below, past empty swings motionless above the rippled sand, seeing the lights beyond, the lights of San Francisco, outside the walls of Homewood.

We skate past the wide steps of the gym, pushing harder now as the driveway rises past the lighted windows of Cottage 24 and Cottage 26, hear rattling of dishes from open kitchen windows, see hydrangea bushes drooping under loads of heavy blooms, past Cottage 42, up and up, to where the forest covers the hillside that rises above Homewood Terrace.

It's dark there, now, under the eucalyptus trees, in the forest where Elaine and I have crawled between stacks of firewood draped with oilcloth, sheltered there, listening to the raindrops splattering above us, smelling the fragrant acorns, snug in our make-believe cottage.

Now the forest is dense and dark and scary, so we skate faster, hurrying back toward the lighted cottages.

Then we're going down, down, gathering speed, hurtling down the steep hill that descends from the forest, the clatter of skates all around me, rattling over the bumpy pavement, a breeze against my face now, a soft touch brushing my skin, overhead slender eucalyptus leaves quivering, black against the deepening sky, my skates ratcheting over pebbly pavement, sending vibrations up my legs and, all around me, scrambling by on noisy skates, the kids of Homewood Terrace.

TWENTY-FIVE

Rose returned to the Kougarok in the spring. On her way to Graff's camp she saw the opportunity she'd been hoping for. It happened accidentally. The bush pilot touched down at Taylor to drop off supplies, the weather closed in suddenly, and they had to spend the night.

Taylor was little more than a name on the map of the Seward Peninsula. There was no town. Only a gravel landing strip, two gold-mining camps, a handful of prospectors working their own claims, and a roadhouse. The roadhouse served Taylor's seasonal population of gold miners as well as a few transients, such as my mother, stopping over on their way to camps farther up the Kougarok.

I don't know how my mother perceived that ramshackle way station in the wilderness as her future, but she said, "I knew it was what I'd been looking for the minute I saw it." She cast a critical eye on the setup. A young prospector, Timmy Sullivan, and his Eskimo woman, Benita Newtak, were managing the roadhouse for its owner, Bess Maggids, who lived in the Eskimo village of Teller and ran a trading post there.

"Timmy was back in the kitchen fighting with his squaw"—my mother said later—instead of selling drinks to the miners who sat playing cards in the front room.

She looked around. If she had the place, she decided, she'd put in a few things for sale. Work gloves, bandannas, in addition to cigarettes and snuff. These were what the men needed, and they'd buy them to avoid the inconvenience of having to send into Nome for every little thing.

There was literally no other place of business at Taylor. If a man wanted a drink, he came to the roadhouse. If he needed a bunk or a meal, or an evening's diversion, there was only the roadhouse. For Rose, remembering the bitter struggles in San Francisco, this was the best part— there was no competition. And it wasn't a nickel-and-dime business, like all the miserable little coffee shops and ice-cream parlors they'd gone broke on. At Taylor, everything was a dollar. A dollar for a shot of whiskey, a dollar for a meal, a dollar for a bunk. Good money.

She talked to Timmy Sullivan, drawing him out about the business. He was happy to accommodate her, even showed her the books. And she realized that he wanted out. Timmy was a gold miner, not a businessman. He had his own claim and a cabin, and all he wanted was to get back to prospecting.

Rose clung to the idea of the roadhouse through that summer, ferreting out whatever she could about it, about Bess Maggids, questioning Graff and the men, thinking, planning, hoping. Here was a business she could handle on her own. Here was something that had the potential of giving her more than wages, something to build on, and, most important to Rose, a place where she could be her own boss.

She worked the season at Graff's camp, not spending a cent she didn't have to. When it ended, she returned to Nome and to Cappy. His father had left town, gone to live Outside, so there was just the two of them now at meals in the kitchen behind the liquor store.

Rose wrote to Bess Maggids and worked out a plan. What the terms were, how she came up with the money, I don't know. She had saved a little—her wages from the camp—but it's unlikely that it was enough to negotiate a lease. Almost certainly, Cappy lent her some cash. Whatever the arrangement, she looked forward to the coming spring, the spring of 1940, when she would take over the Taylor Creek Roadhouse.

Perhaps she planned to leave us at Homewood Terrace until she was settled at Taylor. Perhaps she planned to send for us then, as soon as she felt she had a place to bring us. But that's not quite the way it happened.

TWENTY-SIX

We had been in Homewood Terrace almost two years. I looked forward to the time when I would be, if not a big girl with all the big-girl privileges, at least old enough to go to Aptos Junior High, that white stucco palace on a hill with the flower-strewn wall. If I yearned for my mother, it was to imagine that she lived in San Francisco and took us out on Sundays, just like the other kids' parents did.

Reason tells me that I must have been prepared for what happened next—that Mother would have written us, that Mrs. Gans would have told us. But I have no such memories.

What I do remember—very clearly—is being taken to the Ferry Building by Arthur Osasky. Arthur Osasky, lean and silent and dark. He was the big boy now, now that Henry Richmond had graduated, had a job at Levi Strauss, had never come back to Homewood to visit. Arthur has brought us here, my sister and me, to the Ferry Building, all the way from Homewood on the streetcar. Past the El Rey, past the rows of little San Francisco

stucco houses, with their tiny rectangles of lawn bordering strips of driveway, past the streetcar barn that stands
on top of a hill just before the descent into Market Street,
past the Emporium, where a blind man leans against the
wall with his open box of lavender sachets, past the tall
buildings and empty sidewalks of the business district.
The circle of tracks in front of the Ferry Building is the
end of the line.

It's a huge building, or so it seems to me—like a gigan-
tic shed. Sunlight spilling in from the barnlike doorway.
But inside, beyond that shaft of light, it is dark. It's
hushed in that cavernous space, low murmur of voices
and echoing footsteps on the cement floor. People disappear into the brilliance of the doorway or fade into the
shadows. We hover at the edge of the darkness, my sister
and I, looking into the darkness, waiting.

A ferry docks and we hear it thud against the pilings.
The shadows spew out people. Crowds move around us,
rushing toward the light of the doorway.

Finally, a small woman, wearing an old-fashioned suit
with a skirt down to her ankles, separates from the shadows and moves toward us. She's smiling and holding out
her arms, and she bends down and pulls Lillian and me
against her.

My mother's voice is high and thin and strange sounding. And she has an accent.

And then—all of a sudden, it seems—Arthur disappears. And so does Homewood Terrace and Cottage 24
and Mrs. Gans and Dr. Langer, the poppies and the euca-

lyptus trees. Everything is gone, and Lillian and I are alone with this stranger in a tiny hotel room.

She makes jokes.

"This room is so small," she says, laughing, "you'd have to go out in the hall to make the bed."

She sits on the edge of the bed and pulls me onto her lap.

"Did they hurt you in that place?" she asks me. "Were they mean to you?"

Her questions make me feel all tight and funny, like she wants me to say something bad about Homewood.

I don't know how long we stay there, in that cramped room, the three of us sleeping, head to toe, in one bed. Nor do I remember the train ride to Seattle. But by the time we arrive, my mother's voice no longer sounds strange and I am looking forward to going to Alaska, where there is a lot of snow and where I can have a sled and go sledding. I've never seen snow.

And I remember the pictures from the old album in the trunk in the apartment on Sutter Street. I remember the snow and my handsome father, and I lean against my mother and think about going to this place in the pictures.

And then we are at my aunt Sadie's house in White Center, which is part of Seattle. I don't know my aunt Sadie, because I was only two years old when we left Seattle and went to San Francisco. She is heavyset and has a drooping bosom. She doesn't wear rouge and lipstick like my mother does, and her hair is long and gray and pinned up in a bun at the back of her neck. Her eyes are gray, too, like my mother's, except hers look like she wants to cry.

Mother talks seriously to us. When we go to Alaska we can't ask for nickels and dimes all the time, because there won't be any, she says. And we have to help her, because she is going to get this roadhouse and there will be a lot of work. She doesn't know what a good helper I am now and how I have worked in the kitchen in Cottage 24 and know how to do a lot of things.

So I thought she was taking us with her. I thought we were going to Alaska.

I am sure that she explained everything to us. I am sure that she told us that this time, really, it would only be a lit-tle while, until the First Boat, two or three months. Then she would send for us, then she would have a place to bring us. Then she would have the roadhouse and we would all be together. She must have said these things. But, if she did, the memory was erased by what happened next.

Her reasonable words were wiped out, as were my fan-tasies of Alaska, of being in that place that I knew from the old photo album, the place where my handsome father had dwelled, where my mother and father had been a smiling couple flanking a wicker baby carriage, that place where—finally—I would be, too. They were gone—memories of her words and my fantasies, alike—obliterated by what fol-lowed.

So I don't remember her words. Nor do I remember

that day, that particular day when she went back to Alaska, went away again and left us at the Seattle Children's Home.

TWENTY-SEVEN

There are no landmarks that serve to separate one day, one week from the next. Had an hour gone by, or was it a year? Or was it all a dream? My memories from that time seem secondhand, seem like someone else's memories, seem like events experienced under anesthesia.

The Seattle Children's Home is a large, two-story brick building on Queen Anne Hill. It's divided into a girls' side and a boys' side. But, in my stay there, I never see a boy.

I never hear my name. I know no one else's name. I never touch another person. No one ever touches me. And, in my memory of that time, that place, I am always alone.

I sleep in a dormitory—a long narrow room lined with cots.

There are jobs to do and I do them. I wash a line of toilets every morning before breakfast. I load dishes into metal trays in a big kitchen and push them under a sliding door into a steamy industrial dishwasher, but I can't feel that steam in my face or the cool dampness of the sheets I hang out every day on clotheslines behind the home.

There are other kids there, certainly there are other kids. But they have no names or faces. Except for one. A thin-faced girl with dark circles under her eyes who says that Linda Darnell is her cousin.

And there must be grown-ups in charge. But I recall only one and in only one illuminated moment—when she has yanked my cot away from the wall and I see her arm, an arm so skinny the wristwatch is above her elbow, pointing to the dust balls underneath.

We eat in a dining room with long wooden tables. It is not an unpleasant room—it looks out on a lawn, and a few trees. At the opposite end of the room is a set of French doors, leading out to a hallway.

There is a memory of specific meals. At breakfast, a glass of tomato juice sits by my plate. I must drink it quickly, gulp it down, even though I don't like its strange, thick taste. It's difficult to swallow. But soon someone will come around and pour milk into the same glass. If there is juice left, they will pour the milk anyway. And at dinner what I recall is only a piece of white bread covered with a pale, thick gravy.

The staff doesn't eat with us, they eat at a small dining room on the far side of the kitchen. When I work in the kitchen I see their leftovers—bits of egg on their plates and even meat, which I never see in our dining room. And there is an empty space at the top of each of the big glass bottles of milk sitting on the shelf under the steel tables in the kitchen, marking where the cream has been skimmed off for the staff's coffee.

I am hungry. Some money has been left for us, perhaps twenty-five cents a week. And after school I buy a sandwich, a thin sandwich made of a relish of pickles and mayonnaise. It's wrapped in wax paper, but before I can eat it, I am surrounded by other kids who say, "Divvies on that," which means I have to give each one of them a piece.

Once, I steal food—a loaf of white bread and some sugar—from a storeroom. The gritty taste of those sandwiches remains on my tongue.

On Sundays, I walk to the Christian Science Church, and, on the way, caterpillars drop from the branches overhead and I feel them crunch beneath my shoes.

There are no statues or paintings or colored windows in the Christian Science Church and all the hymns are by Mary Baker Eddy. And someone is telling a story about a little boy who is riding a tricycle. The little boy doesn't see that he is riding toward the edge of a cliff and so he falls over. But all the way down, as he is falling down the cliff, the little boy keeps saying to himself, "I am not going to get hurt." And he doesn't.

I never see my sister. Except once, when I catch sight of her setting tables in the dining room. But when I try to go in, I am stopped and told to write one hundred times "I must not go into the dining room between meals."

I don't know where she sleeps or what her other jobs are besides setting the tables. I can see her, though, see her for that instant, slightly bent over the table. In profile, she is heavy, heavier than I remember her from Homewood, and her cotton dress is tied loosely with a belt. Her nearsightedness makes her seem intent, concentrating on what she is doing. And maybe she is. Maybe she isn't thinking about me, or wondering where I am. Maybe all that she thinks about is setting the table the right way. But I don't know, because she is on the other side of the glass doors, and I'm not allowed to go in.

I never think about my mother or about Homewood Terrace. I never think about going to Alaska. I never cry. I don't even feel the hollow ache in my chest. Everything is dim, seen from a distance. It's as if I am encased in a thick-walled transparent box. Within it, I move around, do my chores, go to bed each night. But I am not here, really, I am just observing this place through the eyes of the little girl who lives in the transparent box.

Except, that is, for one terrible instant. For some reason, I am in the nursery—a separate nursery for the little children (toddlers, really) in the Seattle Children's Home. I am here where these babies are kept, separate from the rest of us. And I am standing at the end of a long hallway, one wall of which is lined with open wardrobes. The toddlers have been readied for bed; they are wearing Dr. Denton's—those cute pajamas with the feet in them. And on the low shelf at the bottom of each stall sits a tiny child.

At the sight of that line of toddlers waiting silently, separately, one to a cubicle, the thick coating beneath which I move shatters.

TWENTY-EIGHT

It was in May—it had to have been May or perhaps early June, although, as I've said, I have no memory of time. At any rate, it was then that Aunt Sadie came to take us out of the Seattle Children's Home. I don't remember the leave-taking, if there was any, nor do I remember how we traveled from Queen Anne Hill to the dock where an Alaska Steamship Line boat lay at anchor. But I recall that she put us on board, gave us a box of chocolates, and then stood waving and dabbing a handkerchief to her eyes as the ship pulled away.

Lillian and I are not surprised to find ourselves on a ship. Neither are we happy or sad.

After the first day, we remain in our cabin, seasick.

The cabin is small and hot and smells of oil. The walls, white metal walls, vibrate with the *thump, thumping* of engines close by. I lie in the upper bunk and whatever I set my eyes on shifts, slipping away from my gaze until I close my eyes to shut out the dizziness, but then the room slides across the black screen of my eyelids.

Lillian lies in the bunk below me, breathing noisily through her mouth. Once in a while she says, "What time is it, Sissy?" As if everything would be all right if she knew what time it was. Or, maybe, she just says it to hear my voice, to see if I am still here, just to make sure. But, of course, I don't know what time it is.

I sleep and waken, not knowing how much time has

passed, not knowing if it's night or morning. Only know-ing that days have gone by in this room.

Sometimes a steward comes, stepping over the high threshold, balancing a tray, smiling. "A little consommé," he says. "Something easy, slides down easy," he says.

Smelling the staleness in that hot, close cabin, leaving the napkin-covered tray.

On the metal ceiling above me tiny cracks like tentacles wiggle out from a large rusted circle. I could turn, turn my head away and look at the cabin, but it's better if I don't, it's better if I lie absolutely still.

Lillian and I hardly speak, but I know she is there, her steady, open-mouthed breathing in the bunk below a com-forting background rhythm.

Once, we pull ourselves, shaky and pale and disheveled, from our bunks and up a metal staircase to the deck. And there's a wet, fishy mist, fresh and cool on my face.

And grown-ups there, strangers who seem to know us. "Rose Silverman's girls," they say, when they see us.

A boy my own age speaks to me, repeating what he must have heard the grown-ups say. "Your mother is the one chas-ing after the man who owns the liquor store," he tells me.

Just saying what the grown-ups say.

And everywhere there's the heavy, rolling sea, and the wooden planks of the deck seem to heave up under our feet.

It's safer in the cabin, in the dark, close world of the cabin. But there the nausea rises like panic in my chest, and time is marked only by the steady thump of the engine.

And then one day the engine stops and it's quiet. Except that outside, on the other side of our cabin door, people are talking in the passageway. Talking and laughing and sounding excited.

Dutch Harbor, they're saying. Dutch Harbor. We can get off the boat.

And we get up and follow them down the gangplank and along a muddy path. It's night and I can't see where we're going. People around me, black shapes on all sides, moving in the dark, and I'm moving with them. It's muddy under my feet, and cold. I imagine a warm place at the end of this path, a place where there'll be hot chocolate. Hot chocolate like we used to have at Dixie Dugan's on Market Street, where Mother took us sometimes, after the movies—to Dixie Dugan's, where a big glob of whipped cream floated on top of the cup, cool and smooth and melting into the velvety warm chocolate.

But we never get to that place. Everybody simply turns around and goes back to the boat.

And then it's a long, long time, days and nights and days again, and the steward comes and leaves a tray and comes again, hours, maybe days later, and takes it away.

And all there is in the whole world is just Lillian and me in this cabin and the stale and rumpled bunks, the white metal ceiling and its rusty spots and the pillow that I turn and turn again to feel its coolness for a moment against my cheek.

And I don't want to go up on deck again; I don't want to see the ocean, to see how big and terrible it is or even think about how it is all around us, and there is nothing else but that gray, black ocean with the endless swells that roll and roll toward you, like a monster that would devour you and drag you down, down so far you can't even imagine how far it is and how dark.

And then some measureless time later when I am asleep or in a dazed half sleep, someone is at our door saying "Get up"—they're saying, "get up, girls."

Because now we're here. And when we go up on deck, everywhere the ocean is quiet and still and pale gray. So pale, so gray that I can't tell where it ends and the sky begins. It is the middle of the night but it is not dark, and there are no stars.

And way down the side of the boat, if you look straight down the steep, sloping metal side, there is a barge full of people, bobbing up and down, and everyone is laughing and waving, smiling at all the people high above them at the railing.

And my mother is there, too, laughing and waving like all the others. I look beyond her to see where we are, but there is nothing, nothing but pale water and sky.

TWENTY-NINE

"What's the matter, baby?" she asks. "Don't you feel good? Are you sick from the boat?"

My mother bends down, and I can see the red splotch

of rouge on her cheek, her floury face powder. Her breath smells like chewing gum. She puts her arms around me and presses me against her rough jacket.

"You'll feel better when you get some fresh air."

I try not to let my face touch her cheek.

We're walking up a dusty road, the three of us. It looks like the outskirts of a town, a few scattered, dilapidated buildings.

But, "This is the town," my mother says, laughing. "This is it."

She is talking and smiling and holding our hands, as if we'd always been here, as if we'd never been in the Seattle Children's Home.

I don't want to be drawn into her warmth. Or maybe I do. In this forlorn place, her nearness is encompassing, consoling.

"You're going to meet someone," she says, smiling like it's a big present.

The Nevada Bar and Grill is full of people celebrating the First Boat. They turn in greeting as we pass the bar in the front room. "Who're the little Cheechakos, Rose?" they ask.

My mother just keeps smiling and holding on to us until we get to a back room, where it is darker and there are tall, stiff-backed booths. Cappy is waiting.

Mother slides in next to him, and Lillian and I sit opposite. Cappy has dark hair and dark skin and his lips turn down when he smiles, but he seems happy to see us, even though he doesn't even know us.

"Have some French fries," he says. "Here, eat something. You look like you could use it."

My mother can't stop smiling, and when she drinks a glass of beer, I think of the laughing young woman in boots and breeches in the old photos, the "straw boss" of the apple orchards.

Later, the three of us go to bed on a fold-out sofa in Cappy's father's house. There are no curtains or shades on the windows, and the room is filled with that even gray light that is the same color as the sea and the sky and all of Nome.

Tomorrow morning early, Mother says, we're going to Taylor Creek.

I don't know where that is or how far it is or how we're going to get there, but too much has happened for me to wonder or ask.

In the morning I find myself next to my sister, jammed into the backseat of an airplane, a very small airplane, between piles of cardboard cartons. Mother is sitting up front next to the pilot. Before we take off she turns and hands each of us a small, folded brown paper bag. "Just in case," she says.

We can't see anything because of the boxes stacked on either side of us, but it doesn't matter because I just want to close my eyes and be somewhere else. The wings are dipping from side to side, the airplane is shaking, and we're rolling back and forth. It drops out from under us and my stomach jumps into my chest and then the plane surges up again and we're tossed all around, and I'm retching so loud and hard that my ribs hurt and Lillian and I are throwing up into the brown paper sacks.

The plane keeps on plunging and then struggling up again, shuddering and vibrating as if it's about to be torn apart. The boxes are crowding in on me, crushing me; the smell of my own vomit makes me retch.

At last I feel the plane making a wobbly descent, and then the wheels are bouncing over a rocky surface. All of a sudden the motor stops, we're standing still, and it's quiet, completely quiet. Except for the roaring in my ears.

THIRTY

When I step down from that plane, step off a narrow metal rung onto a gravel landing strip—sick and shaking and smelling of vomit and wearing my orphan asylum clothes—I see that I'm at the edge of the world. A stark, brown, treeless landscape extends on and on in every direction, stretching up to where the clouds are tumbling across the biggest sky I have ever seen. And the air against my face is pungent and fresh and smells different from any other place in the world.

The plane has come to rest in front of a corrugated tin lean-to that shelters a few rusty oil drums and is topped with a wind sock. Other than that, I can see no houses, no roads, no streets or sidewalks or cars or any sign of a town at all.

A man stands by the lean-to. A man in overalls with thick, cropped gray and black hair and a stubbly face. He grins a gold-toothed grin at Lillian and me, picks up our suitcases, and says, "Watt's my name," and laughs to make sure we know it's a joke.

We follow him Indian file across a footbridge that is only one plank wide and swings from side to side, and just below us is Taylor Creek, which looks like melted ice water and is so clear I can see right through to the bottom.

And on the other side of the bridge is a house—well, not really a house, just a tiny cabin that sits up on heavy wooden skids—and Mother says, "That's where Norma lives," as if this were somebody we knew.

Up ahead, up this dirt path made by tractor treads, a big, black building comes into view. At least it looks big, because there are no other buildings around except for two long sheds nestled close to it. When we get closer, I can see that it's covered with tar paper.

Inside there's a delicious smell of meat cooking, and we go straight back through a long, narrow front room to a big kitchen where a man in overalls and a wool work shirt—a thin, delicate-looking man, whose skin seems stretched tight over his sharp cheekbones and nose—is standing by a large black range in the middle of the room. He glances over at us and smiles the most beautiful smile I have ever seen. His name is Timmy Sullivan, and

Mother explains that he's been "taking care of things" while she was in Nome.

And then she leads us back to the front room and up a narrow flight of stairs. At the top of the stairs is a square, dark, unfurnished space, and through an open door to the right I see a small room with two double bunk beds and, beyond it, another doorway through which I glimpse some cots. "Those are the bunk rooms," Mother says. Then, turning toward the left, she says, "These are your rooms." And there, across the hallway from the bunk rooms, are two rooms right next to each other, one for each of us. Each is furnished with an iron cot and a wooden egg crate and has a long window, through which I can see Taylor Creek right outside. There's a package of new clothes on each cot, brand-new clothes from Sears, Roebuck. I put them on right away and so does Lillian, and hers are exactly the same as mine. Thick rubber boots that come up to my knees and a light blue sweatshirt with a hood that ties under my chin and a pouch in the front to keep my hands warm and two pairs of breeches. I stand there in my new clothes in my very own private room, and I don't want to leave. But Mother says, "Go out and have a look around, kids. Go ahead. You don't have to be afraid of anything up here."

Out the front door of the roadhouse, past a small open area where the dirt is flat and hard like it's been walked on a lot, beyond a stretch of weeds, the ground dips down to a wide bank of bleached pebbles bordering Taylor Creek. Lillian and I stand at the edge of the water with our hands in our pouches. The creek is very wide, and in some places low banks of pebbles stretch all the way across and the water leaps over and around them. The sound of the splashing water is the only sound there is.

Lillian turns and goes back to the roadhouse, but, in my new boots, I wade into the creek, feeling its cold weight against my ankles as I push forward. It's icy clear and shallow. I wade in further where the water's deeper, and it creeps up and splashes teasingly near the tops of my boots, but my legs and feet stay dry and cozy inside.

The water is running fast, and the pebbles on the bottom of the creek, the palest blue and gray and salmony pink, seem to be vibrating.

All around me the water is bubbling over the rocky ledges and skimming the boulders. It parts around my legs, separating and joining on the other side, as if I were a rock, as if I were just another boulder in its path, as if I were meant to be there.

THIRTY-ONE

When I wake up in the morning in my own bed, in my own room, I hear the creek running and the squirrels chattering, chasing each other around the flat, caked dirt in front of the roadhouse. And when I wake up in the morning, I hear pots clattering in the kitchen and I hear my mother cooking, and sometimes I hear men talking and joking because a crew has stopped over and is having breakfast at the long table in the kitchen.

And I pull on my breeches and boots and go downstairs and maybe I'll serve the coffee from the speckled blue coffeepot or bring over the dishes of fried eggs and bacon for the men, who laugh and swear and smoke and rub their stubbly faces and tease me.

At Taylor Creek, there are no rules. None at all. No time when I have to get up or go to bed. No chores that I'm supposed to do. There isn't even any special time I have to eat.

"You don't have to ask me all the time," my mother says. "If you want something to eat, take it. If you want to go outside, go ahead."

But we do chores, anyway, Lillian and I. We haul water from the pond out back in ten-gallon airplane gasoline cans, and stand up on a box to pour the water into the oil drum by the stove. We wash dishes in two metal dishpans—heating the water on the range—and then carry the dishpans over to the counter against the wall. We sweep the old, rotting linoleum on the kitchen floor and the splintery boards of the front room. But when I'm finished with all that, if I start to scrub the stove or the counters like I used to do at Homewood, Mother says, "That's enough, Billie"—calling me by the name she and my father had chosen for me before I was born, when they expected a boy. She always calls me Billie, even though they ended up naming me Julia, after him. I think she calls me Billie because she likes the name, or maybe because my real name reminds her of my father. At any rate, I know it isn't that she really wants a boy—she always says she's glad she had girls because boys get into too much trouble. "That's enough," she says, when she sees me scrubbing. "You don't have to be a slave."

But then I don't know what to do.

Nothing much happens at the roadhouse during the day. Usually, the men don't come by until evening. Lillian and I spend hours playing the phonograph records that are piled every which way on a narrow wooden table near the front door. There must be two or three hundred of them, dusty and scratched, on the table next to a Victrola that has a hinged lid and a brass crank on the side, which has to be wound up before playing each record.

I wonder where they come from, these records. Such a strange mix—old Bing Crosby songs, where his voice is high and trebly, and Kate Smith, too, sounding like a little girl, instead of the fat lady I've seen in pictures. We learn the words and sing along with Bing to "Blue Hawaii," and to Kate Smith's "Dancing with Tears in My Eyes."

There are Irish records—jigs and reels—and songs about Ireland—"Where the River Shannon Flows"—that bring tears to my eyes and make my throat hurt. And songs like "She Thought That She Had Lost It at the Astor," which make my mother laugh, but then she stops and gives us a funny look, as if to say, "What are you listening to that for?"

The best are the cowboy songs—lots of cowboy songs. There's "Old Faithful," where the cowboy sings to his horse ("Old Faithful, we rode the range together; Old Faithful, in every kind of weather . . . ") and "When the Bloom Is on the Sage" (" . . . to be free again, just to *be* again,/When the bloom is on the sage").

As I wind up the handle on the old Victrola, gazing out the side window, I hardly notice the corrugated tin shed or the falling-down warehouse that once was a grand saloon in the gold rush days, because I am far from here, far away, feeling the tropical zephyrs against my face or riding my pony under a "yaller moon."

Sometimes I just sit on the far end of the kitchen range, where it's pleasantly warm under my behind, sit there with my boots braced against the windowsill opposite and stare out at the tundra.

Sometimes Mother asks me why I'm so quiet and aren't I feeling good and do I want something? But I don't know what I'm supposed to say. I do everything she tells me to do and I don't know what else I'm supposed to do.

Lillian sits on her lap, even though she is real big now, and puts her arms around Mother's neck and Mother kisses her, and I don't like to look at them when they're doing that.

It seems as if Lillian just wants to be wherever Mother is and never wants to come out and walk with me or, if she does come out, she'll go a few steps and then turn around.

Sometimes Mother talks to us about the business. She stands in front of the closet in her little room behind the kitchen, stands there with her fists on her waist, admiring the shelves full of shiny bottles of whiskey.

"See that?" she says. "You can get about sixteen shots out of a quart. At a dollar a shot, that's sixteen dollars. Sixteen dollars a bottle and it costs me five dollars. That's eleven dollars profit on every bottle."

I see how pleased she is with the bottles. And I understand. She can make money with them. She tells us how hard it is to make money, to make "a living." That's all she wants, she says over and over—a "decent living" for all of us. And she tells us how hard she tried in San Francisco. How all the businesses, one after the other, went under, how hard it was when my father got sick, how she kept trying, even afterward, on her own. How there was nothing left for her to do, she couldn't make a living, she couldn't take care of us kids, and she was afraid "they" would take us away from her, so there was nothing left to do but to go back to Nome. To take a chance, leave us where we would be taken care of—even though it broke her heart, even though she cried all the way to Seattle—she had to leave us while she "got a foothold." She tells us that even when she went back to Nome, she had to work cleaning houses.

She never minded working hard, she tells us. But you have to have a chance, you have to be able to get ahead. And now, this is it, this is her chance—our chance.

She stands there in front of the open closet looking at the bottles and smiling. I stand next to her and look at the bottles, too. And I understand what my mother is saying.

THIRTY-TWO

The main thing that happens every day at Taylor Creek, if the weather is OK, is the arrival of one of the bush pilots from Nome.

You can hear the faint *put-put* of the motor before you even see the tiny speck of a plane appearing, like a stiff, splay-legged bird, between the hills toward the south, toward Nome. But as soon as we hear it, all of us grab our jackets and head out the front shed and down the tractor path.

After a while, I'm able to tell whether it will be Sig Wein or Bill Munz hopping out when the plane lands, because I can recognize the sound of Sig's little red Cessna or Bill's yellow Lodestar before they even circle the landing strip.

Bill and Sig are about as different as two men can be, I guess. Sig is older. Mother says he's been flying since flying first started, since she was in Alaska the first time, and that was a long time ago. But I think he still likes to fly, because even though he's bald, his round face has no worry lines at all. He wears a cardigan sweater and a wool cap, never seems in a hurry, and leans against his plane and talks and laughs with Mother before he takes off.

Bill Munz is a lot younger and looks like a movie star or, actually, like Dick Tracy. He's tall, has dark hair and a mustache, and always wears a leather jacket and leather boots. He'll say "Hello" and "How are you?" but then he just tosses the stuff for Taylor Creek out of his plane, jumps back in, and takes off.

There's almost always a big cardboard box for Mother from Cappy. It's filled with liquor bottles, packed upright between corrugated cardboard dividers, copies of the *Nome Nugget* wedged in with them, and always, right in the middle, there'll be a long white envelope with Mother's name on it.

She never lets us read Cappy's letters or tells us what's in them. But once I see the words "My dearest angel" in Cappy's big, flowery script.

But Mother talks about him, telling us that he's "considerate," and that's very important. Once she asks us how we would like to have Cappy for a father. I don't know. I don't know what it's like to have a father, except for what I remember about my real father, so maybe it would be all right.

But my real father wasn't "considerate." That's what Mother says. She tells us that he was older than she was and she thought he'd treat her nice because she didn't know about things like what happened when you got married. But he wasn't nice to her at all, she says.

She tells us about how he lost all their money from the North Pole Bakery and Coffee Shop and how, after that, they tried and tried to make a living but couldn't; yet, even so, my father would play poker and lose, but that wasn't what made her mad—what made her mad was that he would be afraid to come home and face her afterward.

Because the worst thing you could be, worse than anything else, was "weak." That was why the bad thing happened with his leg. He made up the pain in his leg because he was too weak to face all the people they owed money to, and if he hadn't made it up, maybe they never would have cut off his leg.

I never tell my mother that I remember him. I never tell her that I remember how I sat on his lap and how he laughed when he told me "the longest story in the world," about the baby bird that couldn't keep up with the flock and fell into a muddy place. And I don't tell her that I remember the feel of his scratchy cheek against mine and the stinging taste of his pipe in my mouth. And how I saw tears in his eyes because I was crying.

Maybe I don't tell her because I'm not sure if these things really happened. Maybe I don't tell her because I'm scared she'll be mad if she finds out that my memories are different from hers. Maybe I don't tell her because I'm afraid she will think that I am just like my father.

Still, I remember the picture of him in the old album. I remember how handsome he was, how handsome and unafraid.

THIRTY-THREE

"Norma's a bad woman," Mother says. "She sleeps with men."

She says this to me, but I know that she likes Norma. They're almost like chums.

Also, Mother says she thinks Norma might be an American Indian, because of the way she looks—very dark skin, a straight, sharp-pointed nose, and jet-black eyes and hair.

Norma used to live in San Francisco, too. But she got drunk in a San Francisco bar one night and woke up the next morning in Reno, married to a stranger who worked for the Alaska Road Commission.

Red Collier is quiet, tall, good-looking, and balding, and he slaps Norma around when he's at home, she tells Mother, with a kind of sideways smile. But he's hardly ever home, because nobody's building any roads at Taylor Creek.

Mother says he probably parked Norma here to keep her away from the bars in Nome. But I'd say his plan didn't work, because he can't keep her away from the roadhouse, where her favorite drink is a boilermaker—a shot of whiskey with a beer chaser.

I spend a lot of time visiting Norma in her cabin. She likes the company. It's just one small room, but she has it fixed up neat and cozy, with the walls painted pale green like an aquarium and a dish rack on a pulley that she can hoist all the way up to the ceiling to get it out of the way.

Over the big double bed there's a tapestry with two rows of medals pinned to it. And Norma doesn't mind when I climb up on the bed to look at them. The medals are swimming awards, and when I turn them over I see her name engraved on the back. At least they have her first name, "Norma," but not one of them says "Collier." Instead there are three or four other last names.

"Do I look fat?" Norma drops her robe from her shoulders and stands in front of me, naked.

I can't take my eyes from the scar that starts just below her full, hanging breasts and runs all the way down the middle of her stomach and disappears in the patch of black curly hair below.

Another day she goes into her bathroom, a little plywood enclosure that has a can with a toilet seat on top, and asks, "Can you hear me tinkle?"

All of this is embarrassing, but I understand that it's about other visitors, not me.

We sit close together at the little oilcloth-covered table at the foot of her bed while she teaches me how to manicure my nails.

"Never, never cut your cuticles," she says, dabbing on the milky cuticle remover and pushing the skin back with an orange stick so you can see the half-moons. Then she brushes on thick, pink cuticle oil and massages it into my nails with the balls of her fingers that feel firm and soft at the same time. I could almost fall asleep while she's rubbing my fingers.

Then she shapes my nails with an emery board, colors under them with a white pencil, and applies clear polish and finally buffs them until they glisten.

Norma holds up both my hands in front of my face.

"There! Now you're a lady. If you just had a little something up here"—she brushes her hand against my chest—"you'd be ready for Freddy."

I would be dying of shame, except there's just the two of us and that's the way Norma talks.

She has a Pekingese named Wah Nee and the malamutes that run loose around Taylor Creek think he's just a funny-looking squirrel, with his smashed-in face and bulging eyes. Norma scoops up Wah Nee when any of the other dogs are around. But sometimes one of the malamutes gets to Wah Nee first and sinks his fangs into the back of the Pekingese's neck and shakes him furiously, the same way they do with the red squirrels. Poor Wah Nee's eyes bulge even further and he looks like he thinks he's a goner, but Norma always manages to snatch him away before it's too late.

The three of us go hiking together on the wet, spongy tundra, and I find that, up close, it is beautiful, with mossy lichens, wildflowers, and grasses of all sorts.

And I feel the chill air, full of rich, musky smells, and we wade into the transparent waters of Taylor Creek to catch sight of a silver grayling or look into the bigger, murkier river, the green and mysterious Kougarok, fearful of stepping in. We might see a beaver there, its ratlike head and round rudder of a tail breaking the dark, slow-moving surface. Norma knows the name of everything—the rosy-colored salmonberries clinging to the low, thick bushes, and the strutting ptarmigan whose feathers change from winter white to summer gray—and she isn't afraid.

Sometimes a weasel springs up from the tundra—a

spindly, terrified thing—stands trembling on hind legs, then slips away suddenly, disappearing into the tall weeds.

We surprise a herd of thin-legged reindeer drifting over a hill. They scatter when we approach, balancing antlers like candelabra on their narrow heads.

The ground is covered with large mounds called niggerheads that you either have to step on top of, from one to the other, or try to walk between. Wah Nee has a terrible time struggling up the mounds because of his short legs, and he pants so hard, his pink tongue drooping out of the side of his mouth, that Norma ends up tucking him under her arm.

The longest hike we take is when we visit Andy Conrad, the hermit. He lives in a sod igloo so far from the roadhouse that he only comes to Taylor once during the season. He stays in that igloo by himself all year long, summer and winter.

I don't know how Norma knows the way to Andy's or even how long it takes us to get there. But when we arrive at what looks like just another tundra-covered hill, no different from all the others we have just seen except for a low, grassy hump, there he is. Andy has a long gray beard, just the way hermits are supposed to, and rotting brown teeth, but, even so, he doesn't look old.

As soon as he sees us, he starts hopping around and jabbering in a language that sounds only partly like English. He grabs our arms and pulls us down the hill to a creek, where he's built a dam out of rocks and chunks of sod. In the middle of the dam there's a doorlike sheet of metal with a chain and bucket attached to it.

Andy splashes around in the water in front of the dam, waving his arms, miming to show us how it works. The bucket hangs over the dam on the "up" side of the creek, suspended by a chain that is somehow attached to the metal door. The bucket is above the water level, and, as best as I can understand through the hermit's gestures and jumbled words, when the water behind the dam reaches it and spills over into it, the weight of the full bucket pulls up the metal door, releasing the water downstream.

Afterward, we climb back up to his igloo and squat on boxes around a burner while he throws some coffee grounds into water boiling in a can and then serves us the bitter black liquid.

He doesn't stop talking, but his words don't seem to make sentences, and I can't really understand what he's saying, even though he winks at me as if I do, except a little bit about a red fox who comes around to visit him.

Norma is very polite and takes the chipped and handleless mugs down to the creek to rinse out before we leave. Andy follows us for a while and is still talking long after we're too far away to hear him.

Later in the season, Andy will show up at the roadhouse, simply appearing out of the tundra—down to get supplies that he'll haul on his back. Hermit that he is, he nevertheless seems to like to be around people, or at least to be around us, because he stays at the roadhouse for several days, spending time with Lillian and me. After a while, I can understand most of what he says.

He teaches us how to cheat at four-handed pinochle, using special signs to let your partner know what your strong suits are. He rubs a finger along the side of his nose for spades, for example, or touches his forehead when he has hearts.

At night I hear him across the hall in the bunkroom, talking to himself, sometimes laughing and occasionally letting out a shout, and I imagine that's what he does when he's all alone in his sod igloo, out there on the tundra.

Now, as Norma and I head back to the roadhouse, his words are cut off by the wind and we have to pay attention to our feet and pick our way over and around the nigger-heads, so I notice the thousands of things growing on the tundra. Nothing grows higher than the stumpy willow bushes, but beneath them you can find clusters of salmonberries and fragile-stemmed wildflowers, bright spots among all the dull yellows and greens of the weeds and grasses.

Suddenly, we come upon four stiff, black-hooved legs sticking up from a shallow ravine. A dead reindeer. We stop at the edge, looking down at the enormous animal wedged into that narrow ditch. Chunks of fur are missing, and its neck is twisted, its antlers caught in the side of the ravine. I know it's dead, but I think for a moment that it might spring up now, pull free its antlers and, giving us a startled look, leap off across the tundra.

But it doesn't move, and we turn away.

We head back toward Taylor. When I look down and see my foot sinking into the soft, squishy ground, and see the endless sweep of tundra all around me, I think: here, where I walk, where I step, this very place might be a place where no one else has ever stepped or walked or been—no one else in the whole world.

THIRTY-FOUR

The men come to the roadhouse in the evenings. Late in the afternoon I start watching for them. Sitting cross-legged on top of the big table by the window in the front room, I look toward Gold Bullion Camp, hidden somewhere behind the hills. I strain to see some movement on the tundra, hoping for something to take shape, to become one of the men I will recognize.

Because when they are there in the roadhouse, everything comes alive. The quiet, shadowy front room fills with men's voices and cigarette smoke, and there's a poker game at the big table by the window. And when the twilight makes it too dim to see by, Mother lights the kerosene lamp, and beneath it there's a warm circle of faces and the clatter of the chips and the soft, intermittent comments of the card players.

So I sit by the window in the afternoons staring at the tundra. I can recognize the men from far away, just by the way they walk. Or by their shape. Or what they wear.

I know John Larsen, slow and awkward, a bulky silhouette loping along the curve of a hill. And Sam Godfrey's hat. No one else wears a hat like that—a fedora—and I know him by his big stomach. Russ Marchon is tall and gangly, his legs like skinny sticks above the bulk of his hip boots, which he wears folded down below his knees.

They arrive, two or three at a time. From either Gold Bullion, behind the rolling tundra a mile or so to the south, or from Keenan's Camp, about the same distance in the opposite direction. And the three lone prospectors— who work their claims by themselves and live in their own little cabins—are regulars, too. There's cross-eyed Kougarok Murphy and there's Jimmy Carroll and Johnny Campbell, who share a claim and cabin.

You can tell they wash up before they come. Faces clean above grimy shirt collars.

Sometimes, there's only two or three—usually the Irishmen, Jimmy Carroll and Johnny Campbell. And maybe they just have a beer or two, swap a couple of stories and leave. But most of the time there's enough for a poker game. And a couple of extras just sitting around watching.

I perch on the stairs, where I can see the game below me. John Larsen's hands are like paws, dwarfing the cards he's clutching. Sam Godfrey, his homely face partly in shadow under his fedora, keeps his cards pressed against his big belly. Slouching with his long legs stretched out to one side, Russ Marchon raises one eyebrow while he looks at his hand, which he holds at arm's length against his thigh.

During a game of stud, my mother's mouth purses while she contemplates first her hand and then the ex-posed cards of the rest of the table. Behind her rimless glasses, her speckled gray eyes narrow when somebody raises her bet and she pinches her lower lip between two fingers and flicks up her hole card with her thumbnail for another look.

She takes poker seriously and judges a man by the way he plays. Kougarok Murphy is a fool, she says. He bluffs all the time and everybody knows it. And he talks too much. On the other hand, Sam Godfrey, the promoter—he musters the money to finance the gold-mining operation—is like her. A conservative player. You can be pretty sure he has good cards if he raises you. But then he can bluff once in a while, because you always figure he has the cards. And that's smart.

You can't trust Russ Marchon. You never know how he's going to play a hand. And there's something about him—something about his insinuating, wide, loose smile—that she just doesn't like.

Johnny Campbell and Jimmy Carroll sit behind the table on the old leather chaise, drinking beer, Jimmy mak-ing wry little observations in his brogue out of the side of his mouth.

The chips clatter onto the table, the dealer's steady pat-
ter is like a chant—"Big Ace; possible straight working;
pair of ladies"—the game's own language.

While Mother plays poker, Lillian and I serve the
drinks. No one asks for just a beer or a shot; they buy a
"round" for everybody.

And, every time, they try to get Mother to have a drink.

"Come on, Rose," they say, "be a sport."

But she never will. She just laughs, or, if she's tired of
hearing it, frowns, and waves them off.

Back in the kitchen I pour beer from quart bottles of
Olympia ("It's the water"). I'm proud that I know how to
tip the glass so there won't be too much head on the beer.

We serve the whiskey in shot glasses, sometimes with a
chaser. The men throw back their heads and toss down
the shots in a single gulp.

When I set the drinks beside each man, they tease me,
grabbing my hand and calling me "Billie the Kid." Then I
go back to my seat on the stairs and watch.

I like the way they look, these men—their rough, red
hands, big and calloused and cut. And the way they smell
of outside and oil and sweat. And the heavy, dark-green
twill of their Filson suits, with its tiny ridges, and the caps
they wear, with the flaps turned up and their skin, with its
rough surface of tiny purple veins and heavy stubble, and
the way they pull a printed red or blue bandanna out of a
back pocket and honk their noses and let their breaths out
with satisfaction.

And I like the way they sit, with legs apart, leaning forward, holding a glass of beer or a shot glass and nodding their heads, and how they tell stories in this easy, laughing way—about the fist-size nugget crazy Andy Conrad found once in the creek where he built the dam, and how he hasn't found even a "color" since, or about how a wolf pack stormed right up to the door of Johnny and Jimmy's cabin one winter, scaring the two Irishmen nearly to death. And I like how they hold their cigarettes between fingers brown with nicotine stains and the way the smoke slips from their nostrils and circles up toward the light.

Sometimes when it's late, Mother turns to me and says, "You getting tired, baby? You don't have to stay up, you know. You can go on to bed."

But I never want to. Never want to miss one moment. How can I tell her that all I want is to be here with the sounds of the clinking glasses and the murmuring of the poker game and the Victrola squeaking out "Sweet Leilani"?

And to know I am here, inside, in the light and warmth, while outside stretches the quiet tundra and the quiet sky.

THIRTY-FIVE

Sometimes, evenings at the roadhouse turn into parties. I don't know how it happens. Somebody'll start dancing, grab Mother or Norma or Lillian or me, and start dancing to the records on the Victrola. Black-haired Russ Marchon in his folded-down hip boots, taking long, wide-legged steps, all loose-jointed, bigmouthed grin on his face, "Goofus" playing on the Victrola.

Sam Godfrey will dance with Mother, never taking his hat off, so dignified, tall, big-bellied, hawk-nosed. He looks off to one side, like he's thinking of something else, something more important than dancing. Mother dainty in her leather boots that lace up to her knees.

Stocky little round-faced Irishman Johnny Campbell wants to teach me how to do the Irish jig. So there we are facing each other in the middle of the front-room floor, him in his hip boots, delicately placing one foot in back of the other, hopping on tiptoes to an Irish tune.

And we all dance the schottische: one, two, three, hop; one, two, three, hop; turn, hop, turn, hop, turn, hop, turn. John Larsen is clumsy but big and strong, and he clutches me around my waist, lifting me right off my feet, right off the floor and spinning me around in the air while the bright fiddle music fills the room, the dark floorboards spring up and down beneath our boots, the kerosene lamp sways on its hook and out the long window the twilight is shifting into dawn.

Murphy, who used to be in vaudeville, announces his imitation of a drunk, which consists of him staggering bowlegged across the front-room floor. "That's some act," Mother says, which means it isn't.

Then Norma decides to demonstrate the hula and she's

wearing a robe—a red satin robe—and nothing else. And she says, "It's all in the hands"—she has graceful little brown hands that she holds up and ripples in front of her face while she moves. And, while she moves, you can see her breasts swinging through the opening in her robe, and she squats with bent knees and says, "Round the island," and she turns, turns, turns, her bare feet sliding against the rough floor, her brown thighs flashing, her rear end swaying beneath the slippery robe.

And later, when the party's almost over, when every man has gone out at least once and stood behind the old warehouse that used to be a saloon but now is just a wreck, stood out there facing the tundra and pissed on the ground between his boots, when Mother's yawning and everybody's kind of quiet but not ready to leave, then, sometimes, Sam Godfrey recites "The Cremation of Sam McGee."

I never heard anyone recite poetry before. Certainly not a grown-up man. Certainly not a man like Sam Godfrey, so imposing, serious, a good card player, respected by my mother, a "promoter," not just a gold miner.

When he stands there in the middle of the front-room floor and looks around, stares everybody in the eye and starts reciting, you can't look away. And the words he says can make you shiver:

"There are strange things done in the midnight sun
  By the men who moil for gold;

The arctic trails have their secret tales
  That would make your blood run cold;
The Northern Lights have seen queer sights,
  But the queerest they ever did see
Was that night on the marge of Lake Lebarge
  I cremated Sam McGee."

But he doesn't just recite the poem, he acts it. He strides across the floor, his Filson jacket flying, building up to the climax, where he flings open the door to our silver-painted, oil-drum stove to stuff in the frozen corpse of Sam McGee.

Later on, Norma asks Russ to "be a gentleman" and take her home. And I watch from the kitchen window, watch them swaying down the tractor path, his arm around her waist, half pulling her along toward the cabin. Alone at the kitchen window, I'm watching. By the time they get to Norma's cabin, through the hazy twilight, they're just a couple of gray specks, but still I see them float up onto the slab in front of her door, and then become one gray speck that seems to melt right into the cabin.

When the last man has gone, pulling the front-room door closed behind him with a soft *squoosh,* Lillian and I gather up the ashtrays running over with crushed cigarette butts and ashes and the empty glasses ringed with foam, and Mother says, "Leave it, leave it. We can do that tomorrow."

But we take them into the kitchen, anyway, and line them up neatly on the counter.

And when I go up to my room, I light the candle that's stuck onto a coffee-can lid, not because it's dark, really, but because I like having the golden flame nearby, the flickering light making shadows that move across the Cellotex walls. Watching them, I fall asleep wrapped in the sweet smell of stale beer and cigarette smoke.

THIRTY-SIX

Two Eskimos, reindeer herders, show up at the roadhouse. I don't know where they came from; maybe they live out on the tundra with the deer. I have never seen them before. One is an old man with thick gray hair that sticks out in all directions when he pulls back the hood of his drill parka. The other man is young and good-looking, the way that young Eskimos are good-looking. A smooth, round, placid face, perfect large white teeth, he is short and muscular.

It's the middle of the day, maybe still morning, but they want beer. They don't talk much, shy, the way Eskimos are, or seem to be. They sit at the front-room table, each with a can of beer, silently. Not glum or stern-looking, just sitting there having their beers.

Then they ask for another round, and another one after that. I'm bringing them the beers, because Mother and Lillian are busy in the kitchen.

Each time they empty a can, they crush it, bending it in half and setting it down on the table. So when I walk across the floor, the cans rock and clatter on the table, and the two men look at them and laugh like children.

Everybody says that the Eskimos can't hold their liquor. In Nome, if a native gets arrested for drunkenness, his name is put on a siwash list—which means that none of the bars or the liquor store is supposed to sell to him.

After a while, they start playing the Victrola, shuffling through the stacks of old records on the table next to the machine. They only like cowboy songs. They find "When It's Roundup Time in Heaven," and keep playing it over and over again.

Mother's fed up. "God Almighty, why don't they get out of here," she says, and makes a plate of sandwiches for me to take to them. "Here," she says, "give them this. Maybe they'll sober up and go home."

The natives accept the sandwiches without any question. The old man looks up at me.

"I know you papa," he says.

I can't believe I'm hearing right.

"Him." He points outside, like my father's out there someplace. "Him, me, boat. Siberia."

The old man lays his hand on my arm, grins at me, nodding his head up and down, like he knows what he's saying, like this is no joke. He knew my father, worked with him, remembers him.

He doesn't say anything else to me, the old man. Doesn't tell me about my father or what he was like, or anything else at all. And then, before very long, or after too long, if you ask my mother, the Eskimos leave.

I don't tell her what the old man said. I don't tell anybody. I just keep it in my heart.

THIRTY-SEVEN

I don't know why I stole the curtains. I just did.

It's kind of a funny idea to have curtains in the front room, anyway. But Mother decides she wants them, and she sends to Nome for some flowered chintz from the Northern Commercial Company.

She and Lillian sew them, making two hems, top and bottom. Then they run a string through the top hem by tying the end onto a big safety pin and feeding it through the opening of the hem, pushing it along through the fabric. Then Mother sticks a couple of tacks in the wall on either side of the window by the poker table and ties the ends of the string around them. I watch the whole thing, see how beautiful the big, rose-colored pattern looks with the light coming through it.

Later, in the middle of the night, I wake up and Lillian

and Mother are asleep and the roadhouse is quiet. And, without even thinking about what I am doing, or having any idea in my mind at all, I go downstairs in my underwear, climb up on the poker table so I can reach the top of the curtains, and untie them. I take them up to my room and, without a thought, stand on my bed and tack them up on either side of my window. Then I go to sleep.

The next morning the sound of my mother's astonished question coming from downstairs in the front room wakes me. "What happened to the curtains?"

Even when I hear her puzzled voice calling to Lillian to come and see, I feel nothing at all. I just lie there looking up at the glowing rosy fabric framing my window. I don't even feel anything when I hear her coming upstairs, Lillian following behind. Or when she opens my door, sees the curtains, and, after a dumbfounded silence, bursts out laughing.

She is still laughing and asking me why I did it as I get up and, without a word, remove the curtains. She and Lillian follow me downstairs and watch as I climb up on the table and rehang them.

For days afterward, Mother keeps telling the story, like a joke, to anybody who comes to the roadhouse, and she laughs and turns to me and asks, "How come you stole the curtains, Billie?" But I have no answer.

THIRTY-EIGHT

You can't see the camps from the roadhouse. But you can hear them when the wind is right, hear the rumbling of Cats and draglines.

Norma and I hike over to Keenan's for a visit. It's not far; there's a path where the grasses have been flattened by the men making their way back and forth from the roadhouse.

But when we come across it, suddenly seeing the pit below us from the rise of a hill, it's as if some monstrous animal has ripped off a swath of tundra leaving a shallow black bowl. Jets of water are dislodging chunks of earth from its sides. And bulldozers clank back and forth across the hole, rolling small mountains of mud toward a dragline's bucket.

Norma and I scramble down the side of the crater, digging our heels in to keep from slipping and then pick our way across the muck. The raw earth smells of rotting things, things that lived and died a long time ago. There are ancient bones here. A mastodon tusk. I saw it myself. Yellow and curved like an elephant's.

We climb the stairs to the sluice box, a long wooden trough tilted high up on a scaffolding. The dragline bucket swings overhead, dripping mud, then dropping its load into the raised end of the sluice box. A fierce column of water blasts apart the mound of dirt and rock, washing it down the trough.

Old Tom Sweeney with his drooping gray mustache is

there, patrolling the sluice box, carrying a short-handled shovel like a soldier on duty. He waves and shouts at us over the roar of the coursing water. Our faces are wet with spray as we watch the pebbles and rocks tumbling down to the edge of the trough, spilling over to the pit below. The gold is there, too, but invisible, clinging to the burlap lining of the sluice box.

Way below us, Lee Schumacher is leaning out of his Cat, waving us down. Next thing I know, I'm sitting high up on the tractor next to him, on a little metal seat. Even though he is Timmy Sullivan's half brother, Lee isn't at all fragile looking like Timmy. Instead, he reminds me of a Dutch boy in a children's book, husky and handsome with bright blue eyes and red cheeks.

Norma is far off, there in the cab of the dragline with Fred Lacey, standing close to him, smiling up into his face, Wah Nee tucked under her arm.

Lee shoves the levers between us and the Cat climbs up a steep hillock and then plunges down the other side, and next to me the churning treads are flinging off mud and I'm thrown backward and forward and lifted up and then slammed down against the metal seat.

Lee looks over at me and grins in a way that is asking, Are you okay? And I smile back and the Cat jolts forward while Lee wrestles with the levers and the muscle pops out on his arm. When he turns to look back, reversing the Cat, his neck is a straight, hard line from his shoulder to the sweep of his jaw.

And I'm bounced up again and feel myself losing my balance and coming down hard against the seat, hitting it so hard the pain shoots up my buttocks and into my back, but not minding it, liking the wind that catches the nozzle's spray and Lee grinning at me, so I just laugh and hang on.

THIRTY-NINE

Timmy Sullivan is a squawman. That's what Mother says. Any man who has lived in Alaska for a while is bound to be a squawman, she says. I wonder if she means my father, too.

Timmy's a squawman because he lived with Benita Newtak right here at the roadhouse, and everybody knows it. Benita's dead now, but, still, he's a squawman. And it's not a good thing to be. Eskimo women aren't like white women, Mother explains. They're "loose." And that's as much as she's going to say about it.

But the fact is, I'm in love with Timmy Sullivan.

Timmy looks so slight and delicate, and his overalls hang loose on his narrow frame. But he's strong as a willow branch, and he can shovel dirt into the small sluice box called a Long Tom and hoist buckets of water all day and never get tired.

But Timmy is different from the other men at Taylor Creek. Maybe that's what makes him a squawman, that difference. But I don't know what it is.

Maybe it's because he grew up in Alaska, in Deering, which is just an Eskimo village. His stepfather, whom he doesn't like, is there. Timmy has brought all three of his half brothers—Lee, Pete, and Donny—to Taylor and gotten them jobs as catskinners at Keenan's. His three half sisters are still in Deering, but Timmy is going to send for them as soon as he can.

Another thing different about Timmy is that he doesn't go Outside in the winter. Or even into Nome. He stays right here at Taylor Creek. Almost nobody else stays at Taylor Creek after the season. Only Andy Conrad, way off in the tundra, and sometimes the two Irishmen. Wien and Munz don't even fly in regularly.

He did go Outside one time. Right after Benita died, Mother says. Went to San Francisco and blew everything he had, just like a drunken sailor.

He never mentions Benita Newtak. Never. But sometimes the men at the roadhouse do. When he isn't around.

"Oh, she had a temper that one." Jimmy Carroll grins and points up at the wall where there's a slash in the Cellotex right over the chaise. "That big, it was," he says, spreading his hands. "Oh yes, a knife, a butcher knife. Stuck right in the wall. Could have been in his head." He laughs.

She seems like a character from a story I've read. Someone made up, not real. I try to imagine her. Squat and dark and wild, in a shapeless calico dress, straight, scraggly hair falling to her waist. Wild and "loose." Except I know she is real, because she has a brother and he's right here at Taylor, working at Keenan's. His name is Smiley Newtak, and he's not wild or strange. He's friendly and has these pointy eyebrows that make it look like he's about to laugh at you, and he does grin a lot, particularly after he drinks a couple of beers.

I visit Timmy Sullivan on his claim, behind the roadhouse, just past the flat gravel stretch and the two outhouses and down a little incline. And he shows me how to pan gold and how to use the Long Tom. And all the time he's showing me, I watch him carefully to see the signs, the signs that say he's a squawman.

I squat next to him beside the muddy pond while he twirls the gold pan round and round, balancing it on his open palms, shaking down the mixture of water and dirt. His slender fingers, pressed against the sloping sides of the pan, are red, blotched with white from the wind and cold water.

"Easy, easy, pardner," he says, when I'm trying it, and his voice is very soft. Is that it? They way he talks, so low and soft? The way his eyeteeth catch on his lip when he smiles and leave two little dents? "Do it real easy."

The gold is heavy, he tells me, heavier than anything else. So you keep shaking the pan, the water sifting and separating the dirt from the gold. Then you tip the pan, ever so slightly, into the pond, letting the water carry out the dirt that's on the surface, but being careful not to lose the gold, which is still hidden in the dirt at the bottom of the pan. Then you dip a little more water into the pan and start again. Twirling and shaking the pan, until at last the gold is washed free of the dirt and the "colors"—thin flakes of pure gold—are revealed in the bottom.

"There," Timmy says, smiling, his sharp, pointed teeth biting into his lip. "There, pardner—see?"

He presses one wet finger against the colors, lifting them up and scraping them against the edge of a tiny glass vial. Then he holds it up and looks at it against the sky.

"That's what it's all about, pardner," he says, and he chuckles, like it's not really important at all. And I am so close to him I can see his black eyelashes wet with the cold mist, and the tiniest purple veins in his blotched, cold-stung skin.

Timmy's cabin is not far from the roadhouse. Not that you can see it from the front room or even the kitchen. It's back beyond his claim, back where the Kougarok bends to the right.

I go there one day when Timmy doesn't show up at his claim. He's sitting up in bed in his long underwear, sick. "Barking like a fox all night," he tells me.

The cabin is dark, a piece of flowered calico covers the window. Hardly any furniture. There's the iron bed, a chair, and a small table covered with canned goods, a pint of whiskey, and a couple of glasses. His muddy shoepacs sit neatly beside the bed.

Maybe I'm not supposed to be here, here where Timmy lives. I never thought of him living someplace other than on his claim. I sit on the one chair that's next to the little table, a wooden chair with a stiff back. The top buttons of his underwear are undone and his chest underneath looks thin and bony.

But Timmy winks at me, just like we were on the claim.

"Have a look," he says, pointing under his bed, where I see the edges of some cardboard cartons. "Go ahead— pull 'em out."

I get down on my knees and slide out one of the boxes. It isn't heavy at all.

"Go ahead—open it," Timmy says.

The box is stuffed full of things wrapped in tissue paper. I unwrap them, one by one, while Timmy watches me from the bed. Little embroidered black satin slippers, painted fans, silky tapestry, a lacquered box with smaller boxes stacked inside. A treasure. I unfold a shawl, rich and lustrous, deep green and scarlet, the edges fringed with silken threads.

"Try it on, pardner," Timmy says. His lips are parted, but he's not quite smiling.

Kneeling there on the floor, I drape the soft, slippery fabric around my shoulders and it slides down my arms and across my chest.

I look up to see a funny expression on Timmy's face. One I haven't seen before. And he doesn't wink or smile; he seems almost to be holding his breath.

"You're gonna be a heartbreaker one of these days," he says.

✳

"Chinatown junk." My mother's mouth turns down at the edges when I show her the shawl that Timmy has given me. "Spent all his money on Chinatown junk."

The man's a fool, she thinks. Like my father, maybe, although she doesn't say it. A fool. As only a man can be a fool.

Upstairs in my room I wedge the shawl into one of the sections of my dresser. Then I lie on my cot and look at its emerald folds—silken, serpentine, mysterious.

FORTY

I go fishing in the Kougarok with Norma. She knows how to do everything—how to bait the hook, pressing the juicy salmon eggs onto the cruel-looking point with its sharp spur that will catch inside the fish's mouth. How to cast a line, whipping the rod back over her shoulder in a wide arc and then flinging it forward, so that the line—so thin and transparent that it's almost invisible—spins high out over the river before dropping in.

We sit on the edge of the bank above the river, quietly watching our lines carried along by the current. The Kougarok is so different from Taylor Creek. As if it is the grandfather, somber and deliberate, and Taylor Creek a noisy, bubbly kid. The Kougarok is dark green, almost black, and moves slowly, silent swirls forming on the surface here and there.

Wah Nee is snuffling around under a willow bush, sniffing some small animal, I guess. I can feel the warmth of Norma's leg next to mine on the rock that we're sharing. She is quiet, her dark profile all sharp angles. When Norma's outdoors, she's different from when she's at her cabin or the roadhouse. She doesn't talk silly, like she sometimes does. And it seems as if we don't need to say anything at all; it's enough to be sitting there watching the green river.

I turn at the sound of a crashing in the bushes, like a reindeer or some other large animal. And I see Barbara Lacey heading toward us. Barbara cooks at Keenan's and is married to Fred Lacey, who runs the dragline. And she's about the only other woman at Taylor Creek. She's big and broad-shouldered, with dirty blond hair, and she's wearing a leather jacket.

Norma turns, smiling and just about to say "Hello," when Barbara comes right up to her, reaches down, and grabs her by the front of her jacket, pulls her up and around, and then flings her down on top of a willow bush.

"You leave Fred alone," she says, standing over Norma, who's sprawled on the bush, still holding on to her fishing rod, "or I'll knock the crap out of you. Understand?"

Norma doesn't even try to get up—she just lies there looking at Barbara, looking really scared.

"Did you hear me, bitch?" Barbara asks.

Norma nods her head and manages to choke out a "Yes."

Then Barbara turns and plunges back through the bushes.

Norma pulls herself up, disentangling herself from the willow branches, and her dark skin is about as pale as it can be. "We're not going to mention this to anyone, are we, Billie?" she says, in a small voice I never heard before.

FORTY-ONE

It is freezing at night, and in the morning the mud puddles are covered with thin sheets of ice. And there's ice in Taylor Creek. At first it's only near the bank, in the little pools that form between the pebbles.

Squatting at the edge of the creek, I poke my finger through the ice and watch the shards twirl away in the current.

The season is almost over. The men will be leaving. Catching the Last Boat from Nome. The camps are quiet. They're shutting down the machinery for the winter.

Mike O'Brien will go on a binge, the men say. Mike, the big Irish nozzle man at Gold Bullion. That's what he does at the end of the season when he gets his payoff, they say. They tell about the crazy things he's done. How he tried to wash his false teeth in the nozzle and how they were blasted so far into the side of the pit he never found them. How he got so drunk that he almost missed the Last Boat and how he had to be hauled on board in the baggage net.

A few people will stay on, spend the whole winter here at Taylor. Timmy Sullivan and Johnny Campbell and Jimmy Carroll. And, of course, Andy Conrad, all alone up there on the tundra. They'll be completely cut off. The bush pilots will just fly over once in a while to drop a few supplies and check to see if there's smoke coming out of the chimneys.

Norma will go back to San Francisco. Maybe she's leaving Red. She doesn't say.

And we'll be going, too. Not Outside, not on the Last Boat, like the others. We're going to stay in Nome.

Mother says that we'll live in a regular house in Nome, it's Cappy's father's house. It has bedrooms and everything. And that Lillian and I will go to school. And that we can go to the movies and that there'll be parties during the winter.

We order school clothes from the Sears, Roebuck catalog because Mother says there's no place to buy them in Nome and that if you do find anything there, it's too expensive.

Mother's in a good mood. After the men get their payoffs, there are a couple of all-night parties. "Made as much last night as I did almost the whole season," she says, the morning after one of them.

Mike O'Brien, who hardly ever came to the roadhouse

during the season, shows up now and gets drunk, just like they said he would—so drunk he can't make it back to camp, and he staggers upstairs to the bunk room.

He lies up there for days, drinking from pint bottles, stumbling down the stairs once in a while, crashing into the walls, just managing to get out the front door before relieving himself. I can hear him at night, there in the bunk room across the landing, groaning and cursing.

I'm scared of him. He's big and his nose is all smashed in, and his face full of purple lines.

Mother says there isn't anything to be scared of. She's disgusted with him, but can't figure out how to get rid of him.

Finally, one day when Bill Munz brings in the Lodestar, two of the men from Gold Bullion drag Mike downstairs and over to the landing strip and throw him in the plane.

Every time that Munz comes in now, he brings supplies that Timmy has ordered from Nome—supplies to get him through the winter. I see him out the kitchen window on his way to his cabin, bent under the weight of the cardboard carton on his shoulder.

"Guess you'll forget all about me when you get yourself a fancy boyfriend in Nome," he says, smiling because he's just teasing.

I know he's teasing, but still I wonder if he really means that he's my boyfriend.

We roll up all the sleeping bags on the bunks upstairs and sweep out the kitchen and the front room one last time. I put away the cards and poker chips in the dark little closet under the stairs.

There are no more poker games, there is no more dancing. Most of the men have left, taking their payoffs back to families, families that I never heard about, never saw pictures of.

For the first time a fox comes right up to the roadhouse. A pair of bright green eyes appear over the low sill of the kitchen window, and then just a flash of orange fur and it's gone, so suddenly, so quickly I'm not sure it was even there.

Soon, Timmy says, the wolves will have the run of the place.

FORTY-TWO

The Last Boat disappears from the roadstead, steaming along the horizon until it's no more than a tiny black silhouette slipping over the edge of the world. Then the Arctic ice pack drifts in, the floes crushing up against each other until the sea is a solid white mass. There'll be no more boats until spring; the only contact with Outside are PanAm's three-times-a-week flights from Fairbanks.

Front Street is dead, deserted. Once in a while, a lone figure with frosted eyelashes and face glazed white from the icy wind passes by the liquor-store window. But most of the time you can look out and see nothing but the oil- or water-delivery truck, tire chains slapping against the hard-pressed snow, or Eli the Scavenger making his rounds with his horse and wagon.

The malamutes roam freely, trotting silently down the center of the frozen street like wolf packs, bunched together, snout to haunch.

Still, it's cozy and warm inside the Nome Liquor Store, especially in contrast with the glacial barrenness of the view out the window. We have our own house, just like Mother said we would, but we eat almost all our meals and spend most of our time at Cappy's store. It's quiet there. Not like the roadhouse, not like the poker games and the dancing and the staying up all night, all the endless twilit nights.

Still, I like being there and I spend a lot of time scrunched up in a captain's chair between the walls of liquor cartons, feeling invisible, watching what goes on in the store.

Cappy calls me Billie just like Mother does. And, just like Mother, he never makes any rules, never says don't do this, don't do that.

I suppose he's good-looking, Cappy. He's not fat or thin. Stocky, really. And he's vain about his thick dark hair. I see him pulling a small black comb through it and smiling at himself in the mirror on the medicine cabinet behind the kitchen door.

His hair may be thick, but his eyebrows are patchy because he has this habit of plucking at them with his fingers when he stands behind the counter, his arms folded high on his chest, chatting with a customer or lecturing a drunk on his lack of self-respect. Cappy himself is a teetotaler. Never takes a drink or smokes a cigarette or uses a bad word.

He wears the same clothes every day, like a uniform—gabardine pants and a gabardine shirt, which is always buttoned up to his neck. Both are the same dark olive color as his skin.

And he likes everything just so. He polishes the liquor bottles and lines them up in perfect rows, pacing up and down the shelves, nudging a bottle that's a little out of line here or not square there.

Cappy has this game that he plays each afternoon: watching the clock to see how long he can wait before he has to turn on the light. It gets dark and shadowy in the liquor store, and he stands there clutching the string from the overhead light, his eyes on the clock in the store window, trying to hold off another minute or two so he can better his record of the day before. Sometimes it's pitch-black by the time he pulls the string, but his smile is triumphant when he announces the time.

It seems as though he likes to have me there, watching him. It feels almost like we're partners, Cappy and I. Especially when he gives me little jobs to do, like pasting the territorial tax stamps on each bottle of liquor. I stand next to him behind the counter, and he sets me up with the big sheets of stamps and a wet sponge in a shallow dish of water. He is patient, he doesn't get annoyed with me, and he shows me the right way to put the stamps on the bottles—separating them into long strips, pulling them across the sponge, and then pressing the stamps, one at a time, onto the bottles. I do it exactly the way he shows me.

When a customer comes in, Cappy introduces me as his "helper."

And I fill gallon jugs with wine from big wooden barrels. First Cappy has to wrestle a barrel over to the edge of the trapdoor to the basement and set out the empty jugs on the stairs below the level of the barrel. Then he starts a siphon with a narrow rubber tube and when he gets a mouthful of wine, he makes a face and spits it out like it was poison. He never lets me start the siphon because he doesn't want me to get a "taste for wine."

I like watching the scarlet liquid bubbling up against the sides of the green glass, and I like the sour, fruity smell.

Each night after we finish the main course, Cappy sends me down to the basement to pick out our dessert. There must be hundreds of cartons of canned food down there. On top of each stack of cartons there's one with a side sliced away as in a display, so you can see what's inside. I wander around, looking at the pictures of pink-tinged yellow Freestone Peaches, the silvery Bartlett Pear Halves, the juicy squares of pineapple, pears, apricots, and the unbelievably magenta-colored maraschino cherries in the Mixed Fruit Salad. I pace between the stacks of cartons, rubbing my arms against the chill, studying all the pictures again, trying to decide which to pick.

But, no matter what I finally bring upstairs, Cappy is surprised, because it always turns out to be just what he had wanted.

FORTY-THREE

Mother tries to please Cappy, to do everything the way he likes. At the roadhouse, she was the boss. In her trim breeches and lace-up leather boots, her flannel shirts, her short, curled hair and rimless glasses, she looked like she meant business. All the men knew it. You could tell by the way they talked to her. They kidded her but not too much, not beyond a certain point, not if she frowned or waved her hand in this fed-up way. She let them know just how far they could go.

It seems that she's relieved, she can relax for a while, doesn't always have to be taking care of things, watching out that someone doesn't step over the line.

When Lillian and I set the table, she reminds us to give Cappy the fork with the bent tines and the stubby little glass that he prefers. And she tells us not to take the heel of the bread at dinner, because that's his favorite.

She cooks the reindeer roast so it's almost raw in the

middle, because that's the way he likes it, and then she slices and slices until she finds the rarest piece for him. They joke about it, Mother and Cappy. "Just warm it up," he says with a laugh.

When I watch him eating the almost raw meat and I see his purple lips shiny from the fat, which is his favorite part, and watch him soak up the bloody juice with a piece of bread, I feel squirmy in my seat. But it doesn't bother Mother, not at all. She smiles and laughs when he says how good it is.

They don't call each other sweetheart, Cappy and Mother. And he never says my dearest angel, the way he did in that letter I saw. They never touch.

Still, I see them standing close together in the liquor store, leaning against the shelves behind the counter side by side, with their arms folded, not saying anything, looking out at Front Street.

There are never any guests at meals, with the exception of Sunday mornings. That's when Cappy makes sourdough pancakes, for which not only we are invited but also any of the liquor-store regulars who happen to drop by. Usually there's Fancy Andy, who comes into the store every day for his bottle of beer. He's small and trim and wears a peacoat; he has a tweed cap over his white hair, and his pants legs are always tucked neatly into the tops of his shoepacs. And he doesn't say much, not much at all.

And there's Russian Mike, who threw himself on his knees before Mother when she returned to Nome, and who has lived in Nome for so long, people joke that he was there when the Russians owned Alaska. He never buys anything at the liquor store but, like Fancy Andy, comes in almost every day. Just to visit. Not that anybody, even Mother, who understands Russian, can figure out what he is saying. He waves his arms and spits a lot when he talks, but the language that Russian Mike speaks is "something else," Mother says.

These sourdough-pancake breakfasts are like celebrations, like a holiday or, maybe, like a sporting event, because for Cappy the most important aspect seems to be keeping score and winning.

While the pancakes are only slightly larger than a silver dollar, crisp and delicate and perfectly golden brown, and served with butter and blueberry jam, I can never eat enough to impress him. "That's all? That's all you're going to have? A measly six?" (Eight, ten, twelve—it doesn't matter how many you manage to put away, the number is paltry in his eyes, and he compares it with his own record, which he seems to set anew each week—eighteen, twenty, twenty-five.) The liquor-store regulars are immediately conscripted into the event, only to fail to impress Cappy with their meager appetites.

He stands, spatula in hand, chiding Mother or Lillian, or Fancy Andy or me, saying, Here, try these, the pan is just right now, these are the best, they're perfect, and everybody is saying, no, no, there's no more room, I'm stuffed, I'm going to bust. The kitchen full of the warm smell of the pancakes on the grill, my mother with her arms folded across her chest, smiling tolerantly at Cappy's boasting, and he's saying, Here, Billie, take this one, this one is the best of all, and maybe then I'll eat one more even though I'm really full, and it is so light, so crisp, it just dissolves in my mouth. And the sun is brushing the fuschia plant, reflecting off my mother's rimless glasses and gleaming on the surface of the white enamel table, around which we sit like a regular family there in the bright kitchen in back of the liquor store.

Yet right next to this sunlit world is the dark cave that is Cappy's bedroom. And on the tall dresser sit framed pictures of his real family. The photographs are like those in old albums, dark and brown and from some other time, long ago. In them, Mrs. Green has a plump, old-fashioned face, and you can just see the fur piece resting on her high bosom. And the children—Mitchell, Miriam, and Gary—with dark, serious eyes, look like grown-ups, look old-fashioned too, like the families you see in those timeworn albums.

They live in Seattle and are "comfortable," Mother says. So comfortable, they aren't interested in ever coming back to Alaska. I try to imagine them in a big brick house with a green lawn all around, sitting in comfortable chairs in their comfortable living room in Seattle, but Seattle is far away from the warm, tidy world of the Nome Liquor Store.

Still, here they are, these framed pictures, looking as if they belong, looking as if they have a right to be here, here on Cappy's dresser.

FORTY-FOUR

As shabby, makeshift, and desolate as it is, Nome looks like civilization compared to Taylor. There are stores and a school and lodges—the Masons and the Oddfellows—and card games and dances at the school gym. Except for the Federal Building, the schoolhouse is the nicest building in Nome. It's a square, two-story, white frame structure with wooden floors and regular classrooms like any other school. It even has a gym.

The school is only three or four blocks from where we live, although part of the way is more like a path than a block. It's not far, but on most days it seems like miles. It's so cold and windy that my face is numb and I walk bent over, behind Lillian, using her as a windbreak. And, all the way to school, I just keep repeating, "Cold, cold, cold."

But it's cozily warm when we get there because the building is steam heated, the only one in Nome that is, except for the Federal Building and the Company Building. Sometimes it's too warm. But the windows are never opened—("Trying to heat the outdoors?" Jonesy, the janitor, whom the kids call Bonehead because he's completely bald, sneers if he sees an open window).

And the dry, overheated air is filled with a nauseating stench. In part, it's the result of the general lack of bathing among the student body. There's no running water in the winter because, they say, Nome is built on a glacier, and there is permafrost, which means the ground is always frozen. So, in the winter, you have to buy water by the bucket from Serge, the Eskimo waterman, who hauls it in a truck from a spring somewhere out on the tundra. At three buckets for a quarter, once a week is as often as anybody can afford to bathe, and sometimes not even that often.

But, mostly, the stink, wafted on the warm and buoyant air, comes from the "chemical toilets" located at each end of the hall. After a while, I don't even notice it.

The grammar school takes up the first floor of the school building, the high school is upstairs. Only white kids attend the grammar school; the Eskimos have a separate school, run by the Bureau of Indian Affairs. But if they go on to high school, they come here.

Because we have moved around so much, I have been to a lot of schools by the time I get to Nome. But none like this one.

All the others had seemed pretty much alike to me. You sat in one of a long row of desks and you did whatever the teacher told you. Sometimes she was strict, like Mrs. White in Redding School where I went when we lived on Sutter. She was tall and large-boned and she taught me—and everybody else in the third grade—to throw back our shoulders, speak loudly, and enunciate clearly so that "the people sitting in the back row of a big auditorium" could hear you.

Or sometimes the teacher wasn't strict, like Miss Duncan at Farragut where I went when I was in Homewood. Miss Duncan was soft and beautiful and wore flowing dresses and a big picture hat during recess. But even in

Miss Duncan's class, everybody sat quietly at their desks and paid attention. And, usually, none of the kids knew one another outside of school.

Every time I start a new school, it takes a while before the teacher realizes that I am the best student in the class, but, sooner or later, she does, and then she has me sit right in front and asks me questions because she knows I will have the answers.

One thing that's different here at the Nome school is that all the kids seem to have known one another for a long time, probably their whole lives, and they even have known our sixth-grade teacher, Mrs. Hartman, and their parents are friendly with one another and with our teacher, too. And they seem to know all about me, even though I just got here. They know that I spent the summer in the Kougarok, that my mother used to cook for Hank Graff, they even know my mother and father lived in Nome a long time ago, when Lillian was born. And they know she works for Cappy. I don't like the way they say, "Your mother works at the liquor store, doesn't she?" as if they didn't know that already.

Another thing is that Mrs. Hartman sometimes forgets about what she is teaching us and tells stories about herself, instead. She tells us that her maiden name was Helen Moore and when she got married the preacher told her husband that he was getting "Hell 'n Moore." She laughs and gets a little red in the face and flutters her hand over her chest when she tells the story.

The kids laugh, too, and then tell each other jokes while

she is talking and they sail paper airplanes around the room, and Mrs. Hartman doesn't even notice.

Most of the things we're supposed to be learning I already know from some other school. But Mrs. Hartman looks annoyed when I say that, and it doesn't seem to matter to her, either, whether I'm an A student or not.

So I'm just quiet, do my work, and spend most of my time at the liquor store.

Except on Sundays, when I go to the Federated Church. There's no synagogue in Nome, of course, and almost everybody, except the Catholics and a few Eskimos who go to small "missionary" churches, attends the Federated Church. It certainly isn't at Mother's urging that I go. Although she believes in God, she doesn't care one way or another about religion. "It probably won't hurt you," she says.

I go to the Federated Church because they let anybody join the choir. And I remember how much I liked singing in the Temple at Homewood. But here all the songs are about Jesus, a name that had never come up in Dr. Langer's Saturday sermons. And although He had figured at the Christian Science Church in Seattle, He seemed a minor figure compared to Mary Baker Eddy.

Now, however, in the hymns I'm learning, Jesus is my close friend—my boyfriend, even. I'm thrilled when I sing "I Come to the Garden Alone," and find out that "He walks with me, and He talks with me, and He tells me I am His own."

Mother says that Jews don't believe in Jesus, aren't even

supposed to say His name. It's something like a sin. Still, she doesn't tell me not to sing about Him.

Cappy, it turns out, is a Christian Scientist. I don't exactly understand it, because he's Jewish, as we are, but then, now I'm a Christian, too. Cappy doesn't go to any church and he never mentions Christian Science, or Mary Baker Eddy, but one time, when I have a headache, he tells me he will fix it and I lie down with my head in his lap while he massages my temples and talks to me quietly and, sure enough, it goes away.

So I attend the Federated Church and sing in the choir and never think about whether I am Jewish or not. But I guess other people do, because, on the morning after Halloween, I find the word "Jew" scrawled on the soaped-up windows of our storm shed.

I don't know if Mother and Lillian see it too. Or if one of them washes it off. But it disappears and they never mention it. And neither do I.

FORTY-FIVE

From the outside there's nothing to distinguish the Dream Theatre from the other wooden false-fronted stores along Front Street. Inside, however, there's a lobby no bigger than five by fourteen feet, with a patch of carpet whose color and design have long since been scuffed away. And there is a noisy popcorn machine with discolored glass, inside of which burns a yellow light giving the impression that the popcorn is buttered.

The theater itself can accommodate perhaps 200 on bare wooden seats, a number of which have missing or broken backs. The Eskimos are restricted to one side of the theater. The reason, my mother explains evenly, is that they smell bad. They don't bathe, and, besides, unlike the white people's furs, their native-tanned parkas stink. Nobody, neither white nor Eskimo, complains or comments on the arrangement.

Friday is cowboy night at the Dream Theatre. Gene Autry or Roy Rogers and the Sons of the Pioneers. Saturdays feature big musical extravaganzas, and Sunday there's a mystery or romance. I've already seen many of the movies years ago in San Francisco.

Scratched, faded slides advertising local businesses like the Nome Drug Store or Polet's or the Northern Commercial Company are projected before the film starts, while the audience, bundled in parkas and mufflers in the stuffy, rank room, call greetings to one another and laugh and joke until the movie begins.

On Friday and Saturday evenings there are two showings at the Dream Theatre—one at seven and one at nine. Lillian and I go to the early show and Cappy takes Mother to the late one.

By the time he brings her home, my sister and I are upstairs in bed. I have my own room, but it has no bed, so I sleep with my mother in a double bed, the only furniture in her room besides a galvanized tin water tank. Sometimes I'm asleep, but sometimes I'm not. Then I hear the front door open and close and I lie listening to Cappy and Mother talking in the living room. I can't really hear what they are saying, just the low murmur of their voices back and forth.

I strain to hear, to know what they talk about when we aren't around, what they say to each other when they are alone, late at night, downstairs in the house. Are they sitting across the room from each other? Or close together on the old couch? I lie stiff and unmoving under the quilt, tensely aware of eavesdropping on something forbidden.

After a while, I no longer hear their voices. Only quiet from the living room. Yet Cappy must still be there. I haven't heard the opening and closing of the front door.

I'm rigid with the strain. Why aren't they saying anything? What's happening? The quiet seems to extend for a very long time and I get scared, as I used to when I waited for Mother to come home to the apartment on Sutter Street.

Then I start to cry. Loud enough so that she eventually hears me sobbing and comes upstairs.

"My side hurts," I tell her when she bends over me, looking worried and annoyed at the same time. Sometimes I do have a dull ache in my right side and maybe I'm having it now and maybe it's appendicitis and maybe my appendix will rupture and I'll die. Then she goes down-stairs and I hear murmuring and the front door opening and closing and then she brings me up an aspirin and comes to bed.

Finally, after one of my attacks, my mother asks me if I want to see the doctor. I think she hopes I'll say no, because she doesn't like doctors after what happened to my father. But I am afraid that maybe I really do have appendicitis. So we go.

The doctor is an old man who says he doesn't know for sure if I have appendicitis but he'd better operate "just in case."

So I find myself in Nome Hospital. I have little memory of the operation itself, but afterward my stomach seems to be on the move, shifting from one part of my body to another, and I ask my mother if I'm going to die.

Russian Mike comes to visit. He bends over my bed, his face close to mine, spraying me with his spittle. I understand not a word, but I like the way he touches my hand when he talks, and, before he leaves, he reaches under the layers of clothing he wears and finds a present, which he presses into my hand. Afterward, I see that it is a package of dried herring.

Mother brings me ginger ale, which tastes better than anything I ever drank and promises me I can have a birthday party if I want. When I am out of the hospital, Cappy says that I have put my mother "through hell."

He is mad at me, it seems, but I don't even care. It feels

good to know that my mother worried about me, that she felt bad about my being in the hospital, that maybe she was even afraid that I would die.

FORTY-SIX

The temperature climbs to zero, and everyone says spring is here. On sunny days when the wind doesn't blow, people push back their parka hoods and stop to talk to each other on Front Street.

The snow, piled higher than my head on either side of the street, begins to melt, revealing layers of soot and dog excrement. Here and there, sidewalk planks are visible beneath the crusted snow.

There's mention of the First Boat, although the sea ice looks as solid and impenetrable as ever. All over Alaska, bets are taken on the date of the breakup, the day the ice will flow out of the Nenana River in Fairbanks.

Mother says it's time to get ready to open the roadhouse for the season. School won't be out for another month, but we can take our textbooks with us and send in our work. That means we'll miss the arrival of the First Boat, we won't see the barges plowing back and forth all day and night between the boat and the jetty. And we won't be there at the post office with everyone else, watching and waiting for the treasures from the First Boat. Nor will we taste the fresh fruit, precious and rare and yearned for all winter, which, for a little while at least, will be for sale at astronomical prices at the NC store.

And how will Cappy get along without us? He will have to cook his own meals, eat by himself at the dinette, go down to the basement and pick out his own dessert, wash his own dishes. But if all this bothers him, he doesn't show it. Nor does Mother seem anything but happy looking forward to another season at Taylor Creek.

It's business. And business always comes first. If there is something important besides business, besides earning a living, it isn't something you can talk about.

After another nauseating, wrenching plane ride, Bill Munz drops us off at Taylor. There is still snow on the ground and the creek is frozen solid—so solid that we walk across from the landing strip instead of taking the footbridge.

The days and evenings are long and quiet before the full crews show up at the camps. To pass the time, I explore the old saloon, the crumbling building that stands, or barely stands, just beyond the front door of the roadhouse. It's the only structure left over from the gold rush that began in Nome forty years ago and spilled out over the Seward Peninsula as far as Taylor, where there was a boomtown of several thousand people.

Now the long, low building is too dilapidated to be used, even for storage. But a fine wooden bar is still intact, although the floor it stands on is nothing more than dirt.

Beyond the bar, there's an opening to what might have been a gambling room. Today there are only damp and rotting beams and a ladder leading to bare rafters overhead.

At the top of the ladder, in wooden cartons balanced between the rafters, I find what is left of the old settlement. Crawling on all fours from plank to plank, I stop to pick through the contents of the boxes. There are dishes and pans and glasses. Some shredded rags of clothing, a few still recognizable as baby clothes—all of this suggesting a Taylor far different from the one I know, a Taylor I can't even imagine.

And there are books. I find a spot with enough flooring left to sit on, prop my back against a wall that has a small, dusty window, and browse through the selection. There are books with warped, water-streaked covers, with pages stuck together, pages with dried flies pressed flat inside. Books with very small type and chapter headings that begin with words like "Wherein"—"Wherein Toby finds his fortune hidden under a tree . . . "

Did children grow up here, at Taylor? Did they read, as I do, by kerosene lamp or candlelight? Had their families struck it rich, these long-gone prospectors? Alone in the ruins of the old saloon, I rummage through the remains of strangers whose names no one remembers, whose histories no one has recorded.

I bring some of the books over to the roadhouse and Lillian and Mother and I lie in the bunks in Mother's tiny room behind the kitchen, laughing while we read Booth Tarkington's *Penrod* and *Penrod and Sam* out loud to each other, finding the author's tongue-in-cheek recounting of the exploits of the little Hoosier boys hilarious. Mother laughs so much that her eyes tear and she moans and says, "Stop, my ribs are killing me." And we, convulsed as much by her uncontrollable laughter as by Penrod, say, "Ma, your ribs can't feel anything," and, gasping, she says, "Oh yeah, then how come they hurt so much?"

And we're all there in the double bunk bed in the tiny room, Mother and me crowded together on the bottom and Lillian on top, and there's no one else around, and nothing but silence beyond this room, and so it seems like it is the whole world.

The men return to Taylor, but not Norma. The little cabin on skids is empty, locked and boarded, and I wonder if the tapestry with the swimming medals still hangs on the wall over the bed and the glasses remain in the rack that pulls all the way up to the ceiling.

Timmy Sullivan is here. But something is different. Maybe it is that I am not quite a child anymore. Not that I understand much about the mysterious something that happens between men and women. I have only my mother's vague warnings about men. They always want something from a woman, she says. Something, by implication, that a woman doesn't want to give, isn't supposed to give.

Certain things begin to happen that I don't understand, yet sense their meaning enough to recognize that I am coming dangerously close to the mystery.

There is Bert's hat, for instance. I remember only that he was stocky and dark-haired and worked at Keenan's. His hat is wool plaid and, like Sherlock Holmes's hat, has a beak in both front and back. I'm intrigued by that hat and he offers to give it to me, but there is a condition. I have to come over to Keenan's to get it.

When I find him at the camp, he leads me to a tent where a warm, soft light filters through the canvas and we stand on a wooden floor and I see that he likes me, because he wants to hug me and he pulls me up against his big chest and I feel his warmth and closeness and his scratchy man face pressing into the side of my neck and he asks me if I want a "hickey," but I don't know what that is. He draws back, takes his arms away, and moves off, looking at me like he is surprised by something I said or didn't say. "You really don't know anything about it, do you?" he says.

I know enough not to tell my mother.

And then one day I find myself alone in the front room with Ray Petersen. Ray Petersen who scares me a little. Because I have heard the story about him, about the dog team he borrowed from Tom Sweeney.

The men say it happened one winter when the two miners were both wintering over at Taylor. Ray borrowed Tom's dog team for a trip into Nome. He stayed longer than he said he would, but, worse than that, when he finally returned to Taylor Creek, the few dogs that were still alive were nearly starved to death.

The story went that Tom Sweeney, although already an old man, called Ray into his cabin, shut the door, and gave Ray a thorough beating with a pickax handle.

And now he is here, in the front room of the roadhouse, slinky and lean, narrow-eyed, with a yellowish cast to his face. Why are the two of us here, alone, in the afternoon?

I am playing records, leaning on the closed top of the Victrola, and he stands opposite me, smiling his smirky smile. His hand, with index finger extended, reaches across the top of the Victrola toward me. And then the tip of his extended finger traces the outline of a flower printed on my sweater right over where my breast would be, if I had breasts.

Only that moment, brief, loaded, unsettling, remains, and it becomes another of the pieces of the puzzle that I keep in a secret cache—Cappy and Mother, Norma and Barbara Lacey, the big girls wrapping pads at Homewood Terrace, Mother's warnings about men.

FORTY-SEVEN

The war coincides with my puberty. Almost immediately, it seems, everything changes. Alaska is "strategic." The Japanese might invade any day.

The gold mining shuts down, the men have gone to war,

the machinery to the war effort. The roadhouse is out of business.

We won't return to Taylor Creek.

In Nome, Chief Yaeger blows the firehouse siren and says it's a practice air-raid warning. I sit in my mother's lap and tremble. She shakes her head and says she never thought she'd have to live through another war.

A new picture of Gary, Cappy's youngest son—wearing a flyer's cap, which makes his face look longer and thinner—appears on the dresser in Cappy's bedroom.

Suddenly, there are throngs of soldiers on Front Street. They wear long woolen overcoats and little overseas caps, which leave their ears exposed and ready to be frostbitten. Their faces are soft and clean-shaven, and they look stunned, vulnerable. There is no base or barracks for them. It's winter, and all they have are tents thrown up on the beach and out on the tundra. You hear stories about frozen toes and noses. You hear stories about suicides.

The soldiers crowd into the bars, the Polar, the Nevada, and Jin's. They all have Southern accents. At the liquor store they ask, "What do you do around here?" They can't believe, can't comprehend the desolation. Cappy smiles and shrugs his shoulders, like they are too dumb to explain things to.

He rubs his hands. He's selling liquor so fast that he frets he'll run out before the First Boat.

When spring comes, the army builds a big landing field just outside of town, and a base full of Quonset huts. One of them is a theater, where they show brand-new movies, and others are an officers' club, an NCO club, and a PX. Front Street rumbles with army trucks and jeeps and something called a Weasel that has both wheels and treads. And there is even an army radio station, where we hear Eddie Cantor and *The Make-Believe Ballroom* and *The Hit Parade* on the new long-playing records.

The town is full of strangers. Generals come to inspect the base. Mysterious civilians on secret missions to who knows where are seen and then disappear.

Once the ice goes out, the roadstead is dotted with black silhouettes. Every morning from the upstairs window of our house I see the outline of another freighter on the horizon. Merchant marines, sailors in peacoats and bell-bottoms, and regular marines in their handsome green uniforms with red stripes on their arms join the soldiers looking for excitement along Front Street.

They line up outside the liquor store, get drunk, and fall into fights in the mud, to the delight of the little Eskimo kids who stand watching until the SPs and MPs arrive with billy clubs swinging from their belts.

Then the Japanese really do invade, landing on Attu and Kiska, at the end of the Aleutian chain. It won't be long, everybody thinks, before they will be in Nome. I read stories in the *Reader's Digest* about Japanese tortures—a water hose up your nose and worse things. Most of Nome's white families leave for Outside.

Still, the town is frantic with activity. Red Cross workers—women in sensible shoes, short, fitted jackets, and overseas caps on bobbed hair—open a recreation center, a prefab wooden hall right on Front Street.

A short, misshapen woman with a pockmarked face, a barrel chest, and skinny legs appears and starts what Mother calls a "sporting house" in one of the cabins on a back street.

Russian flyers, wearing long tunics and leather boots and smoking filtered cigarettes, which no one had ever seen before, buy everything Cappy will sell them, even grain alcohol. Russians, they'll drink anything, Mother says. She knows. She had lived under Russian occupation for a year in that other world war. The foreigners laugh in surprise when she speaks to them in their own language. They sweep up all the goods at the NC Store, too—everything they can find, because you can't get anything in Russia, Mother tells us.

The American soldiers make fun of the "Russkies." They are lousy pilots, they say with a laugh. Cracking up the American planes they are supposed to ferry to Siberia before they are even off the runway.

I am twelve. A merchant marine invites me to the movies. My mother looks worried.

"It would be okay if all they wanted to do was hug and kiss you," she mutters. But she doesn't say what else they want. And she doesn't say "No."

So I go to the Dream Theatre with the merchant marine. He is nineteen, and his hair a dense black thicket. When he puts his arm along the back of my seat, I lean forward to avoid his touch.

All I know about sex is what I have gleaned by inference from Mother's complaints about my father, about his demands. When she says their marriage had been "ten years of hell," I understand that no normal woman would enjoy this bestial thing men demanded.

What is clear, unmistakably clear, is the horror of pregnancy. Pregnancy outside of marriage, of course.

Amazingly enough, it isn't uncommon, even in Nome. It happens that girls get pregnant when they aren't married. Not regular girls, of course. There has to be something wrong with these girls. They are "tramps" if they are white or "loose" if they're natives. You are just born that way, although that doesn't keep you from being responsible for it.

And, once it happens, there is no undoing the consequences. There are women in Nome, even mothers of girls I go to school with, married women whom everybody in town knows had gotten pregnant before they were married. Everybody knows about it and it clings to the woman like an aura—this hidden, dark thing. Some part of her must still be like that.

Mother tells me in whispers about the mother of two of my classmates in school, who (and she drops her voice and gets this little smirky smile on her face) had been "wild" when she was young, not the respectable lady she likes to present herself as now, with her gray hair worn up in a braid across her head and her glasses, her knitting, and her matronly figure. Oh no, that's not who she really is.

And the Eskimo girls—well, never mind about them. They just don't know any better. Get pregnant and don't even try to hide it or anything. They have the babies and somebody takes care of them and that's that. It doesn't seem to make any difference to them or to their families, or anything. They show off the babies just like a married woman would!

Sometimes a girl just disappears—a white girl, that is. Goes Outside to "get a job" or "go to school." And that is the end of her. You never hear about her again. Although occasionally a baby appears, sent back by the exile, presumably, and then the grandparents in Nome raise him and there is no explanation, no rumors, at least none that filter down to my level.

Yes, one thing I know. Getting pregnant is the worst thing. Everybody would know what you are. Would know it for the rest of your life.

FORTY-EIGHT

The handsome captain asks a favor. The High Holy Days are coming up soon. It would mean so much to the Jewish boys on the base if they could have services in a real Jewish home.

As if the Jewish holidays mean anything to my mother. As if she even knows when they are.

"But he was so handsome in his officer's uniform," she says, flushed and glowing like a girl, "that I said okay."

And then she begins to enjoy the picture of herself as gracious hostess. She wears her dress with the sequined bodice, small pearl earrings, her short hair tightly curled, a little extra rouge making spots of red on her cheeks. Smiling and welcoming the dozen or so Jewish soldiers, who look awkward and oversized in our small living room.

The handsome captain leads the services and we sing the special holiday song, "Ein Keiloheinu," that I remember from Homewood Terrace. Afterward, he makes a little ceremony of presenting Mother with a compact engraved with the date and with thanks from "the Jewish boys of the Nome Air Base."

Flattered and expansive, she, who has never invited a single guest to our house, opens her arms and says they are all welcome at any time, that they should consider our home as their home.

Private Steiner shows up the next evening. And then regularly once or twice a week thereafter.

We are sitting in the living room, Mother already with her hair in pin curls, settled in with a book, Lillian and I reading, too, or doing homework. And Steiner arrives. After all, he had been invited.

He's from Brooklyn. A lump of a guy, with little to say and less humor. He has taken her literally.

Mother tries to make the best of it.

"Where you from? Oh yeah? Brooklyn? What do your folks do?"

It quickly grows thin, and Lillian and I don't say a word. But it seems Steiner doesn't notice, or doesn't expect

much, because he appears at our front door on a regular
basis.

Mother groans when she sees him approaching, watching him head doggedly along the side of the Federal Building toward our house. "What am I going to do with this
guy?" she says, laughing at the pickle she's gotten herself
into, but nevertheless annoyed.

Catching sight of Steiner approaching one evening, she
falls to the floor on all fours and waves at Lillian and me
to do the same, so that we are below the level of the big
front windows through which he would be able to see us.
"Come on," she whispers, and starts crawling toward the
kitchen.

The three of us creep across the living-room floor on all
fours. When we reach the kitchen, Mother opens the door
to the deep closet that runs beneath the stairs and gestures us in. By this time, Steiner is knocking on the front
door. Crouching in the closet, one in back of the other, we
hear him calling, "Mrs. Silverman, Mrs. Silverman."

My mother is squatting behind the closet door, holding
it open a crack so she can peek out. "Beat it," she says
under her breath.

We can hear Steiner's footsteps, then, along the plank
walkway that skirts the side of the house. He is coming
around to look in the kitchen window.

"Uh-oh," Mother says, and pulls the closet door closed
toward her. In doing so she loses her balance and falls
backward, knocking over Lillian, who is crouched right
behind her, and Lillian knocks me over, so that the three

of us are piled up on the closet floor in a jumble of rubber boots, mops, and brooms. Thrashing around in the dark, we start to laugh and, at the same time, try to stifle it, which, of course, makes us laugh even harder.

When we finally crawl from the closet, weak and teary-eyed, Steiner has disappeared.

FORTY-NINE

One or another of the army units sponsors a dance every Saturday at the school gym. They send printed invitations, string crepe-paper streamers from the balcony, and hand out dance cards to the girls.

I discover Max Factor pancake makeup, just like they use in Hollywood, and it makes me look like I am sixteen. I buy a long taffeta dress at the NC store and an artificial gardenia to wear in my hair.

Scores, maybe hundreds, of soldiers stand around the edge of the dance floor, rocking back and forth, eyeing the twenty or thirty eligible "women." They constantly cut in on each other, so that I never finish a dance with one partner.

Invariably, there's a fight because someone refuses to relinquish a girl. "Why don't you step outside?" one of them says to another. And then the gym empties out as dozens of soldiers rush outdoors for the only physical contact they are likely to get. It's exciting, the fighting. Fighting over women, fighting over me.

Sometimes a soldier holds me especially close, his hand firm against my back, and I don't even know his name, and we don't speak, but we move together to the music and for those moments there isn't anything else—not the gym, or the Eskimo kids scurrying and sliding between the dancers, or the other couples bumping into us, or the dingy, treeless town outside. There is just the moist warmth of his cheek against my face, the pressure of his hand flat against my back, his thigh brushing mine, and the way we move just right with the music.

I meet Wilson at one of the dances. He is so tall my forehead rests against his chin.

"Can I carry you home, sweet thing?" he asks.

He is from Arkansas. His first name is Lamar, but I never call him anything except Wilson.

He's tall and skinny and pimpled, Wilson, and has thin blond hair with a single wave in front. Still, he has a sweet, flirtatious smile, clear blue eyes, and a short, narrow nose.

He is twenty and I am thirteen. Of course, I don't tell him I am thirteen, and I like to imagine that he doesn't know.

He comes to see me several times a week, and sometimes we go to the Dream Theatre. When the lights go out, Wilson holds my hand and traces a circle around my palm with his finger or strokes the flat inside of my wrist. Entire scenes transpire on the screen without my noticing, but when the lights come on and the gleaming white nightclubs and lamé evening-gowned heroines are replaced with the Dream Theatre's bare floors and broken seats and the audience of shapeless bundles shuffle out onto Front Street's mud and false-fronted shacks, I feel ashamed.

My shame deepens when, as we pass the Federal Building, Smiley Newtak, good-natured Smiley from Taylor, presses his face against the jail bars on the second floor and calls out my name in a cheery greeting. I put my hand through Wilson's arm and pretend I don't hear.

On the evenings when we stay home, the four of us sit around the living room, Mother and Lillian on one side reading, Wilson and I talking on the couch, pretending that we aren't excruciatingly conscious of their presence. It would be better if Lillian had a boyfriend, too, but she doesn't date, doesn't go out. She could if she wanted to, there are so many soldiers, and I don't know why she doesn't. It just seems like she only wants to be with Mother.

I can't begin to imagine what Wilson and I have to talk about. I am always tensely aware of the need to skirt any subject that involves chronology. It seems to me we spend several evenings discussing how sharp the creases in his pants are.

But the tension is really about when my sister and mother will go upstairs to bed so that we can neck. It becomes a silent battle between their resistance and our determination. We always win.

I sit on Wilson's lap and we kiss for hours. Then it doesn't matter how old I am. Nothing matters but the feel of his hard, skinny thighs under my rump and the delicious taste of tobacco in his mouth. Not even the fear of getting pregnant penetrates the delirious oblivion of his kisses. It's only later that I worry. I don't know how a baby happens. Maybe French kissing can do it, or maybe touching my breasts stirs up something. Maybe it happens like spontaneous combustion.

Still, when we're kissing, I have no sense of the passing of time. Except—oh, humiliation—when I hear my mother's voice, cold with anger, calling to me from the top of the stairs, "Come up to bed, Billie."

Wilson leaves quickly then, not making it any worse for me than it is, and I go to bed and Mother lies there with her back to me, saying not a word. The next day, she speaks to me only if she has to.

I'm not at all sure what forbidden line I have crossed. I have heard Mother call certain women "tramps," and she has told me that Norma was bad because she went to bed with men. But I haven't gone to bed with Wilson. Maybe it has to do with how late I had stayed up with him alone downstairs. But hasn't she done that with Cappy? There is no way I can find out for sure. I don't dare ask, for fear of her answer, for fear of being branded with a name that I could never get rid of, for fear of finding out the truth— what I am really like, what really is the name of the terrible thing that is wrong with me. For fear of being cast out.

I keep a diary and report conscientiously on the major

war news ("Allies still eighty miles from Rome"), the top songs on *The Hit Parade* ("I'll Walk Alone"), and books I am reading *(Magnificent Obsession)*. But in the corner of each page, in a little code I've made up, I note the number of times that Wilson kissed me the night before.

FIFTY

I am awash with the newly discovered joys of necking, the memories and re-creations of which fill my mind too much for me to be aware of anything else—certainly not the unlikely possibility that my mother has an emotional life of her own, the nature of which I can't even imagine.

I spend the days remembering Wilson's kisses and the evenings waiting for him to return. I never know in advance when he will get a pass from the base. Toward evening I stand at the upstairs window, peering into the darkness along the side of the Federal Building—the direction from which Wilson will appear, if he is coming. I strain to see the tall, skinny form in the long overcoat separating from the shadows. I might wait for an hour at the window, concentrating on the darkness, as if I can will him to emerge through the sheer force of my eyes. Finally, I hear my mother calling from the living room, "Billie, what are you doing up there?" although I'm sure she knows very well, and I am suddenly aware of how cold it is in the unheated room and of the darkness around me.

So I go downstairs, where Mother and Lillian sit reading and I feel whatever warmth there is drain away at the prospect of the long, silent evening.

My mother's cold and wordless disapproval of what happens between Wilson and me down there in the living room, her tone of disgust when she refers to the thing that all men want, her contempt for "loose women" and "tramps," lend more confusion to the puzzle of her "real" relationship with Cappy.

Cappy goes Outside to "visit his family," for a month or so. And Mother, then, watches the store. Who is this family that has call on him, that lives so far away, never comes to visit, is nothing more than photographs on his dresser?

Surely Mother isn't satisfied with being forever the "other wife," the butt of the town's gossipy jokes. Maybe that's why she never socializes. She has no friends, she confides in no one. Oh, she exchanges all the small talk when she passes people on Front Street or over coffee at the North Pole Bakery. She smiles and cracks jokes, but no one ever comes to dinner, we are never invited to anyone's home for a party or a meal.

She seems so self-contained, calm, unperturbed. She must be confident that she will get what she is waiting for. On the other hand, my mother believes in, and preaches to us, the dangers of getting your hopes up. "Don't get too excited," she says, if I am looking forward to something, maybe even a party dress I've ordered from Sears. It might not come, it might not be what I had ordered. Besides, it's not that important. You have to guard against disappointment, against hurt, and, above all, against sadness.

If she has hopes and expectations, my mother keeps them to herself and shows no outward signs. Does she even permit herself to feel how empty the store is when Cappy is gone? Does she even miss the dear, comforting sameness of his routines, his banter with the regulars, the game he plays each evening with turning on the light?

In the gloom of the dimly lit store, where the darkness comes so early now, I feel that familiar falling away in my chest.

Sometimes I lie in Cappy's murky bedroom, that shadowy cave, on the old iron bedstead, the sweet, coconut scent of his hair oil clinging to the ragged throw. With the faint sounds of a pan rattling in the kitchen or the *ding* of the cash register from the store just at the edge of my consciousness, I drift off into daydreams of Wilson.

Once, as I lie there on Cappy's bed, staring at the ceiling with unfocused eyes, my hand brushes against something under the edge of his pillow. I pull on it and a magazine appears. It is open, folded back to a full-page picture of a woman. She is wearing heavy lipstick, smiling, smiling right at me. She is smiling even though her blouse is unbuttoned, completely open, so that her great, white, naked breasts, which point in opposite directions, toward the edges of the page, are exposed.

I quickly slide the magazine back under the pillow.

Cappy's family is looking down at me from the top of the dresser.

FIFTY-ONE

I'm going to miss you, sweet thing, Wilson said. Giving me a heart-shaped locket with his picture. To wear around my neck.

We had been seeing each other for a year. A year in which Wilson had come to dinner, sitting down with us in Cappy's kitchen, neat and tall and blond, and saying "Yes, ma'am" to Mother and "Yes, sir," to Cappy and I could see they liked that, and seeming sure of himself and, after all, he was a sergeant, and making me feel important because he was there, there because he wanted to be with me.

A year in which he took me dancing at the NCO club just about every Saturday, where the other soldiers could see that I was the sergeant's girl and where, when we danced, my forehead rested on his smooth chin, fresh with aftershave, and, I knew that, later, after the dancing, would be his kisses.

Now he was gone. He'd been "rotated." That's what happened in the army. And that's what they all want, the soldiers in Nome. To be rotated out of this hellhole, this end of the earth, this nowheresville. Rather be in god-damn combat than in this hellhole.

Wilson said he would write to me once he got there, wherever "there" was. But he never said we'd see each other again. He never said the word "love." I don't know what that means, anyway. I only know the weeks turned on those evenings when he appeared out of the black shadows edging the Federal Building, the outer rim of his ears bright red with cold, and I felt the cold clinging to his rough wool army coat, smelled the fresh laundry scent of his shirt with its regulation three creases along the back, noticed the neat way his pants legs were folded over and tucked into the tops of his shiny, lace-up leather boots.

I only know I liked his kisses. I liked to be close to him. To feel his skinny shoulder through his shirt, to stroke the taut muscle along the back of his neck, liked the way his small white teeth and parted lips so close to my face were blurry and out of focus. His soft southern accent asking what I wanted when I pushed closer to him, and my not knowing what he meant or what I wanted, other than to be where I was, close to him, close to the warm, intoxicating mix of aftershave and tobacco.

He is gone and I still do everything I always did. I go to school, I come back to lunch at the liquor store, and after school, too. I siphon wine for Cappy and help my mother grating potatoes in the kitchen. But there's this hollow, achy feeling in my chest, like the feeling of those afternoons in Homewood Terrace when I watched the huge gray bank of fog advancing across the sky over the playground.

I do everything I am supposed to do, but sometimes

now I just stand at the kitchen window staring out at the mud-colored breakers endlessly spewing pale foam along the narrow beach.

"What's the matter with you, Billie?" my mother asks, if she finds me standing there, staring out the window. "Why are you mooning around?"

Is there something the matter with me? Besides that my chest feels funny, this empty feeling again, like there is a hole in it? I don't know why I stand looking out the window. I just watch the waves, one after another, watch the way the swell begins to build, way, way out from the shore, a slow heaving, as if in pain, and gather fullness as it moves headlong toward the beach, until it seems it can hold no more as it curls, lifting into a heavy roll, and finally lets go, breaking in a long, diagonal line of fragile gray lace that is immediately sucked back into the sea, to begin the slow, unchanging process all over again.

"If you keep mooning around like that," Mother says, "I'm not going to let you go out with soldiers anymore."

The ice pack drifts in, stilling the restless sea. The vast white wilderness appears solid, immovable, endless. Yet one morning I will wake up to find that it has disappeared overnight.

Sometimes Eskimos venture out to its edge, to where the ice gives way to open sea. Go to hunt for seal and walrus. And sometimes they are lost, stranded on a floe that breaks off from the pack, and they drift out to sea.

The shoreline edging the frozen landscape consists of a narrow, rocky strip of beach bordering the back of the buildings that face onto Front Street. It presents a vista of rotting boxes, scrap lumber, rusted oil barrels, dilapidated sheds. There isn't a tree, not even a barren branch to add a graceful line to the dismal scene.

I stare at the bleak landscape as I stand at the sink doing the dishes. Right next door, behind the police station, a white malamute is tied by a short piece of rope to the handle of a shed door. They're rounding up strays, now. The police holding the animals until somebody claims them. The dogs are too dangerous, it is said. No one has been bitten, no one has been attacked. Still, they can't be allowed to run loose anymore, they can't be allowed to run in packs.

The dog is asleep, curled into a tight circle, its snout tucked under its tail, its fur matted with dried mud. There is an enamel dish nearby, so the animal has been fed.

Malamutes are part wolf, they say. Long snouts and long, lean bodies. They don't bark like regular dogs. They howl like wolves. When the fire siren sounds, its wail is echoed by a heartbroken chorus throughout the town.

I see the malamute stir, raising its head, as if disturbed by a sound or perhaps sensing something moving nearby. But everything is quiet, so it settles back into its circle.

As I wash the dishes, I go over the work I'm doing in my head, as I always do, as if I were reading an instruction book. The glasses come first, dipped into the warm, soapy water. Then the silverware, then the china, and, lastly, the pots and pans. There is a good reason for the order. The

greasiest things left for last, so that the glasses and silverware are greaseless, spotless, sparkling. It is the way I had
learned in Homewood. I always review the procedure in
my mind, repeating it to myself over and over, even
though it's something I know by heart; something I do
well.

Out the window, the dog tied up behind the police station is awake. Awake and sniffing the air. Someone is coming. Chief Yaeger is making his way along the alleyway
between the liquor store and the police station. He isn't
young, Chief Yaeger, and he is heavy and tall and wears a
belt cinched below his belly, with a holster and pistol on
one side.

The malamute is up on all fours now, alert, its ears
forming two erect triangles. It lowers its head and its tail
wags harder and harder in excitement, pulling its rear end
from side to side. The rope digs into the dog's fur as the
animal strains forward toward the approaching man.

Chief Yaeger stops about three or four feet in front of
the dog. His large hand goes to the holster at his side and
he slides out the pistol and stretches out his arm. The tip
of the gun is almost touching the animal's head, just
above its eyes. Then he fires.

The gun goes off. The malamute's body leaps full length
into the air, the rope pulling its head back, its body twist-
ing like a hanged man. Its wildly rolling eyes look right at
me. They are terrified, terrified and bewildered.

After the shot, not a sound anywhere. Yet I'm trembling

from its reverberation. I hold onto the edge of the sink, staring out the window where the malamute lies on the ground, a piece of crumpled fur.

I see Chief Yaeger stoop and untie the rope that is pulling the dog's head up at a strange angle, so that it has a puzzled, questioning look. I see him grab a handful of fur, swing the carcass back and forth to get momentum, and then fling it wide, letting it fly far out over the embankment onto the frozen sea. It will stay there until the ice goes out in the spring.

My mother finds me sobbing on Cappy's bed. At first she tries to comfort me. Tries to make little of what I have seen. "You can't get upset like this, Billie," she says, sitting on the edge of the bed, her hand touching my back. "You can't cry for everything in this world."

But I keep crying, even though I know she wants me to stop. I can't stop. I don't want to stop. Even though it feels as if my ribs are crushing my heart.

My mother turns away from me. The anguish frightens her, but I don't think about that, I don't know about that.

"What's the matter with you, getting so upset," she says. "It was just a stray."

I am lost in the crying, in the sting of tears on my cheeks, on my lips, in the shiver of cold tears coursing down my neck.

I don't know what I am crying for. For a stray dog. For Wilson, for my father.

I press my face into Cappy's pillow, damp now, and cool against my cheek.

FIFTY-TWO

How much was happening that I didn't know about? How much was secret, hidden? What storms, worries, fears, indecisions, transpired behind my mother's unshakable façade?

Suddenly—very suddenly, it seems—she leaves. Flies to Fairbanks to "see a doctor." She who so distrusts doctors. There have been no signs of illness, and she doesn't say what the problem is. Nor does she explain why she would travel some 500 miles to see a doctor when there is one in Nome.

She's gone for three weeks.

At the same time, Cappy is Outside, visiting his family. For the first time, the liquor store is closed.

It's spring, school is out, and Lillian and I are usherettes at the Dream Theatre. We don't think too much about what Mother is doing in Fairbanks. She told us. She's seeing a doctor. Besides, she sends us notes saying she's "feeling better" and she thinks "the treatments are working." Don't worry, girls, she writes—just take care of each other.

Like everyone else in town, we are waiting for the City Water to come on. That's when we'll have running water for a few months. Won't have to buy it from the water truck, three buckets for a quarter, like we do in the winter, and we can take baths more often than once a week. Every morning the first thing we do is turn on the faucet over the big galvanized metal storage tank in Mother's bedroom to see if the water has started yet.

In the evenings we go to our jobs at the movie house. On Fridays and Saturdays, I work the early show and Lillian works the late one. Mother has left us some money, so we eat most of our dinners at the Nome Grill or the North Pole Bakery and Coffee Shop.

One evening I come home after the early show to see water seeping out from under the front door of our house onto the plank sidewalk. For a dazed moment I ponder the sight, thinking, That's funny—water usually runs from outside in.

When I open the door I step into a pool of water that extends across the entire living-room floor. Water is pouring through the ceiling, and great, flat sheets of it are sliding down the walls, splashing onto the floor.

I slosh through the kitchen and on back to the stairway, which has become a waterfall.

By now I understand. We left the faucets open. The City Water has started.

Panting and sobbing, I fight my way up against the torrent and into the bedroom, where water is gushing over the top of the storage tank. I turn off the faucet and run, soaked, half sliding down the stairs, out the front door, along Front Street to the Dream Theatre and my sister.

I am crying so hard it is difficult to choke out the news—the house is flooded, the house is flooded.

My sister, in her neat white dickey collar over a navy blue sweater, her usherette's flashlight poised, looks at me. "I'm working," she says.

I turn and run back along Front Street. I begin bailing

out the living room with a kitchen pan, water still dripping from the ceiling and down the ruined wallpaper.

I am bailing and crying when Sam Godfrey appears at the front door. It was unusual for him—or anyone, for that matter—to drop by our house. How he happens to be there or why he has chosen this moment to come to our house is a mystery.

"Is Rose home?" he asks. "Thought I might get up a poker game."

He doesn't seem to notice that I'm crying, that I'm barefoot and my pants are rolled up to my knees, or that water is dripping from the ceiling into a large pool on the living-room floor.

"No," I say, "she's in Fairbanks."

He nods, tips his hat, and walks off.

The next day, Lillian and I go over to the Signal Corps office in the Federal Building and send a wire to Mother. "Everything fine. Don't rush back."

By the time she does return, we have managed to dry out the carpet, but there's nothing we can do about the stained and buckling wallpaper or the oil stoves that no longer work. But she hardly seems to care or, unbelievably, even to notice. She is thinking about something else.

Shortly afterward, when Cappy returns from Outside, we find out what that is. Mother tells us we're leaving Nome—we're moving to Fairbanks.

FIFTY-THREE

"The town's booming," she says. "There are opportunities there."

We are leaving Nome, just like that. As if our life here, our life with Cappy, counts for nothing. We're going where she can get her hands on some of that easy money that is circulating in booming, wartime Alaska. That is enough explanation.

At least, that's how I understand my mother's decision. But I don't understand very much. There is, it would seem, a very different scenario being followed, a secret one.

In Fairbanks, we don't need to look for a place to stay. Arrangements have somehow been made before we arrive. We have a room in the house of a couple named Kaufman. Who they are, how Mother knows them, or why we are staying there, I have no idea.

There is something different about the Kaufmans. Particularly Mrs. Kaufman. A woman of perhaps fifty, she speaks with an English accent. She seems educated, but she is unkempt—without makeup, her long, gray-streaked hair ungroomed and pinned loosely in a bun. She shuffles barefoot across the dirty linoleum floors. She speaks of a daughter, a grown daughter who is a doctor.

Today I might see her as a Bohemian, a freethinker, perhaps even a radical. Not someone who, in the normal course of things, my mother would know. At the time, however, I didn't wonder how they were acquainted.

Her husband seems a background figure, in bib overalls with a cap topping a pink, cherubic face.

Our quarters—a windowless, cheerless room at the rear of the house—has a separate bathroom and entrance. There are three single beds, each placed flush against a wall. We take no meals with the Kaufmans. We see them infrequently.

Beyond our colorless room, the town itself is exciting, abuzz with activity. As Mother said, Fairbanks *is* a boomtown. Even more than Nome. The entire Territory is on military alert. A war zone, now that the Japanese occupy two islands in the Aleutians. Fairbanks is the hub of an enormous military effort.

There's a sprawling air base, and the small town is overrun with military personnel and with civilian engineers and construction workers drawing down big money fast. Overtime, double-time, triple-time. And with young women up from the States, clerical workers, lucky enough to be the right age to get the good-paying jobs at the base, giddy with the excitement of being so far from home, of so much money, of so many handsome, unattached men.

There is a shortage of everything. Especially help. Lillian and I have jobs within the first week. She is sixteen and can type. She is hired by the army. At fourteen, the best I can do is a job as a waitress at the Co-op Soda Fountain.

Meanwhile, Mother is looking around for "opportunities." Or so I thought.

I am soon caught up—or, rather, overwhelmed—by my

new job. At the Co-op, I work one-third of the long, U-shaped counter. There are never enough seats, never enough help, people are clamoring for more coffee, more soup, a clean fork, ordering soda-fountain drinks I've never heard of, have no idea how to make.

I am slow. I deliver the wrong orders. I forget the water, the bread, the coffee refill. The customers are always angry.

"Don't they have child labor laws in Alaska?" a soldier asks, unsmiling.

I pray no one will sit at my station. But it is constantly jammed.

The two other waitresses on my shift are of little help. Ruth, the older one, is terse and professional, wears white shoes with thick crepe soles. Calves stringy and hard. She makes a brief effort at training. Shows me how to balance three dinner plates along my arm, tells me never to move without carrying something—a dish back to the kitchen, glasses of water out to the counter—instructs me in the foreign language in which I am to speak to the cook: "Boil four on two," "Whiskey down," "BLT to go." But it is busy and Ruth has little time to waste on some fourteen-year-old dumbbell. Besides, there are good tips to be had if you hustle.

The other waitress is a big southern girl with long curls who has followed her soldier boyfriend to Alaska and is too dreamy, distracted, and in love to pay attention to me.

My biggest problem at the Co-op, however, is not the other waitresses or the irate customers, but the cook.

The cook. Six-foot-two and lean. Swathed in white. Keeping a dozen orders straight in his head. Maybe two dozen. He is charged, jittery—a high-voltage wire arched over the spitting grill.

Next to him is his girlfriend, whose fat white legs end in black pumps, her high heels hooked over the rung of a stool. She sits next to the stove, close enough for the cook to fondle her between flipping hamburgers.

His narrow, angled face tenses as I fumble over my orders or when I can't recognize the dishes that he slides on the stainless-steel shelf. "Pick 'em up," he hisses. I dread having to ask him to redo an order on which I have erred or seeing his about-to-erupt expression when I struggle to remember how to call in the orders. Once, as I stand with my back to the swinging door, watching him slam down the patties on the grill, stammering through my recitation, he suddenly turns and, in one swift, unbroken motion, flings a raw potato at my head.

When my shift finally ends, I slip out the back door of the Co-op, my feet swollen, my apron greasy and stained, my hair limp with sweat, to the room behind the Kaufmans' house just across the street.

One day—it must be a week or two after we arrived in Fairbanks—I encounter a man carrying a small black satchel leaving our room just as I am entering. "Kidney stone passing," he mumbles, without looking at me, without stopping.

Inside, my mother is lying under the covers, her face turned to the wall. She is moaning.

"Go away, Billie," she says. "I'll be all right. Go away."

Afterward, Mother makes no mention of the incident, and, as far as we know, she continues "looking for opportunities." What she actually is doing during the day, when Lillian is working at the base and I at the Co-op, I don't know. Perhaps she tells us about a Laundromat she's considering, or even a shoe shop. Something different, she might say, maybe I'll try something different, not a restaurant, not a coffee shop. Although I know what she really wants is a liquor store, like Cappy's. What a business, she would say. It's so clean, no dishes to wash, no help to give you headaches and steal from you. And the profit. You sell a bottle of scotch and, just like that, you make maybe four, five dollars profit. No work, no mess. But liquor licenses are expensive and not easy to get.

Maybe she considers all these things as she looks at the throngs of "transients" the war has deposited in this town, all with high-paying jobs, thinks about the money they're itching to spend. She just needs the right spot.

Or maybe she has no intention at all of staying on in Fairbanks. Maybe she spends the entire day sitting with Mrs. Kaufman in her dreary kitchen, talking of who knows what.

However she passes her time, not long after the day when I had encountered the man with the black satchel coming out of our room, Mother tells us that she is going back to Nome. She is going back to Nome, but she is leaving us behind. "You girls better stay," she says. "Lillian has to work out her contract with the army."

She doesn't say anything about her "illness" or about what had happened to her plans for a new life in Fairbanks. Nor does she say when my sister and I should come home or, for that matter, how we are to get there.

Mother leaves us in each other's care. That's what she has always told us. We're responsible for each other. Except, of course, Lillian, being older, is really the responsible one. When we are on our own, when my mother is not there, my sister assumes her protective role. She doesn't tell me what to do or boss me around, she is as "hands off" as Mother. What she does do is start planning immediately for our return to Nome. Without acknowledging that Mother has said nothing about how or when we are to get back, Lillian checks the airlines for their fares to Nome and advises me that we have to save everything we possibly can from our salaries so that we can pay for our tickets. Meanwhile, we stay on alone in that jumpy, overwrought town full of strangers, stay on alone in our dismal room.

Once, Mrs. Kaufman invites us into her kitchen. A dark, unpainted, dingy space. Her feet are streaked with dirt up to her ankles. She seems distracted, not there. She drops two teabags in chipped cups and covers them with tepid water, feels along a shelf for a package of crackers, but finds nothing to give us.

Mostly, though, it is just the two of us.

Each afternoon, I wait for Lillian to come back from the base and we go to a coffee shop for dinner. We scan the menu for something we can afford. Everything is inflated in wartime Fairbanks. Just order an appetizer, Lillian tells me. She is determined to get us back to Nome, whether Mother wants us or not. Not that we ever say this out loud—that this time she may have left us for good— something we never even consciously consider. But, in fact, Mother sends us letters discouraging our return. "No point in you girls rushing back here," she writes. "Nothing much going on in this town."

Behind her glasses, my sister squints her pale blue eyes; she presses her lips together. But we never question why we have been left.

After dinner, we go back to our room.

Life in Fairbanks changes with the arrival of Audrey Gundersen, a sixteen-year-old girl whom we know from Nome. A quarter-breed Eskimo, she has blue eyes and a little upturned nose. She dresses in short skirts and wooden clogs, and her curly blond hair is cropped in a stylish "victory cut."

She has joined the USO Club, she tells me. Had to lie and say she was white. Why didn't I join? I could lie and say I was sixteen.

So I become an official USO hostess.

The USO Club is just a shell of a building. One of the temporary army structures. But there is music, a card room, a Ping-Pong table, a big lounge with soft sofas and chairs and a whole wall of windows, so the room is full of brightness.

And young soldiers—a steady stream of them. Square-shouldered, trim-haired, eager, dark-eyed, blue-eyed, southern accents, Brooklyn accents, good dancers, smooth dancers, awkward dancers. Different every day. Young boys, really, but they seem worldly to me. A twenty-eight-year-old sergeant is "the old man." Some are on leave from the Aleutians. Tough duty. Most barren, godforsaken, windswept, desolate spot on earth. To them, Fairbanks looks like Paradise.

And, to them, I look like a woman. They want to dance with me, to talk, play cards. Be with me.

When I'm not at the Co-op, I'm at the USO.

What a warm place it is! How warm it is in the arms of the young soldiers! How they hold me close, smile at me, tell me I am pretty, what a good dancer I am, what a surprise to find someone like me in this god-awful place.

I forget about Nome, I can bear the Co-op. I spend my wages on new dresses. A long gown with a fluffy net skirt printed with flowers; a brown wool jersey dress with a bodice studded with gold nailheads.

Lillian never complains about my spending all my time at the club, or about my buying dresses instead of saving money for our tickets to Nome. While she doesn't date and she doesn't join the USO, we still eat our meals together, spend every night in the room in back of the Kaufmans'. Maybe it is because of my sister's benign and steady—if remote—presence that I am able to forget our abandonment.

Like a homing pigeon, Lillian checks the airlines, trying to make reservations for Nome. But she can't. All flights have military priority. No telling when there'll be seats for civilians.

It is well into September before this interlude ends, as abruptly as it began.

An old bush pilot named Archie Ferguson leans over the counter at the Co-op.

We don't know Archie—he flies out of Kotzebue, a tiny Eskimo village about 200 miles north of Nome, above the Arctic Circle. A grizzled old bush pilot, built like a boxer, short and bowlegged, a fringe of cropped, rusty gray hair around a face so weatherbeaten his eyes disappear in the wrinkles.

"Your ma told me to pick you girls up," he says. "Don't waste any time, I gotta take off before the inspector checks my load."

The leaving is so unexpected, so sudden, that there's no chance to think about the USO Club and the dancing and my beautiful dresses. Just the scramble to get ready. It is time to leave, Mother wants us back. Has found a way to get us back.

And we're on our way to Nome. Retching and vomiting in Archie's overloaded, rolling, churning, tossing, dipping, shuddering plane. We are finally over Nome when he turns and shouts above the roar of the propeller, "Socked in. Going to Kotzebue."

Two more miserable hours before we're bumping along a barren landing strip. In the overcast, a few Eskimos stand at the edge of the strip, summer calico drill parkas glued to their bodies by the wind, silently staring at us.

Shaky-legged and sour-mouthed, we follow Ferguson to a roadhouse amid a smattering of shacks. Inside, an Eskimo woman wearing a loose cotton housedress, her hair in a long braid, comes forward. Archie's wife.

She points upstairs to a room, where we find a bed and nothing more. Lillian and I sit on the edge of the bed, not wanting to lie down on the damp blanket. Cold, shivering. A windowpane is missing.

Then the woman calls us into the kitchen. It is warm and fragrant with a wonderfully delicious and unrecognizable aroma. The oilcloth-covered table is set for the two of us. I didn't know I was hungry, hadn't realized how long it had been since I'd eaten, until I taste the rich, fishy, dark and exotic meat of the wild duck the Eskimo woman serves.

She stands at a distance and watches us eat.

From the next room, I hear the shuffling of mukluks across a wooden floor and the whine of a cowboy song on the Victrola.

The following morning, Archie Ferguson flies us back to Nome.

FIFTY-FOUR

"I hope you kids aren't mad at me, acting so crazy." That's what Mother said in one of the letters she'd sent us while we were in Fairbanks. Trying to explain her erratic behavior, she had cast it in terms of making a living. Things were slow in Nome, she had written. Maybe she'd return to Fairbanks. She wasn't sure what to do.

But it must have been more than that. "Crazy," she had said, "acting crazy." Distraught was more like it—frantic, even. Surely, there had been a crisis, something so disturbing, so unsettling that it breached the steady, near-impervious façade she had maintained for so long.

But I didn't even guess what that crisis might have been, what might have shaken her so deeply, until some thirty years later. Then a clue simply appeared, literally fell into my lap, in the form of a letter printed in a magazine. When I read it, I could finally conceive of the link among the abrupt and bewildering events of that strange summer.

The letter was about abortion—a proabortion statement—the writer identifying herself as a longtime crusader in the fight to legalize the procedure. She had been a feminist, she wrote, long before the term existed. I read the name printed below the letter: Etta Kaufman, Etta Kaufman of Fairbanks, Alaska.

Mrs. Kaufman! Mrs. Kaufman of the distracted manner, the dirty feet, and unkempt hair. Mrs. Kaufman, to whose house we had come as strangers. And to whose house, too, had come the man with the black satchel who had left my mother moaning and with her face turned to the wall.

Here, at last, was evidence of the real relationship between Mother and Cappy. The truth, or the possibility of understanding, after all these years. Pregnant. It would have been her worst fear come true. A shame and humiliation she'd never outlive. This visible sign that she had submitted to the dirty, disgraceful, forbidden thing. No, maybe not submitted—maybe wanted it, enjoyed it, even needed it. Now they would all see. Now they would all know.

And now she was dependent on Cappy to make good on his promises, for surely there had been promises. Only if Cappy could marry her right away could she hope for some pretense of respectability. Perhaps that explained Cappy's trip Outside, perhaps he was trying, really trying, to get free. And perhaps he had failed and then there had been nothing left for her but the frightening, degrading alternative—the "treatments" that didn't work, and, finally, Mrs. Kaufman and the man with the satchel.

She was alone, alone with this calamity. And for once her feelings were stronger than she was. Overwhelmed, frightened, desperate.

Who knows why she rushed away to Fairbanks or why she then rushed back. Why she left us. All I know is that this time her resolution, her stoicism failed her.

Yet her return to Nome must have given her some hope, once again, for a future with Cappy. Because by the time that Archie Ferguson managed to fly Lillian and me back to Nome, whatever the issues had been, they seemed to have been resolved. At least, to all outward appearances, our life there looked a lot like it had before.

FIFTY-FIVE

Maybe they could have worked it out, somehow. Maybe we all would have lived together in old man Lowenstein's house. Cappy and Mother and Lillian and I. Maybe I would have had my own bed in my own room and Cappy and Mother would have slept in the big double bed in the room with the water tank. Maybe we all would have walked to the store together in the morning. Cappy and Mother in front, Lillian and I following. Right down Front Street, where everybody would say "Good morning," or "Cold enough for you?" And then we'd all have breakfast together in the bright kitchen in back of the store.

But it didn't go like that. Because there was to be at least one more event in this secret scenario.

I become aware of it when I come "home" to the store for lunch and find the shade drawn on the glass door and a sign, quickly scrawled with a marking pen on the back of a piece of corrugated cardboard, wedged into the side of the glass: CLOSED DUE TO BAD NEWS.

Inside the darkened store, Mother stops me before I can go back to the kitchen. "Gary's missing," she says.

Gary, Cappy's younger son. The flier. Missing in the South Pacific.

She sends me away. "Go get yourself a sandwich," she says, handing me some money. I'm not to see Cappy that day.

When I do see him, perhaps a few days later, back at work, he is standing in front of his shelves, staring at the empty counter, his patchy eyebrows pulled together in a frown, as if he is trying to figure something out. When customers come in, he waits on them as usual, reaches for a bottle, slips it into a paper bag, takes their money, and rings it up, but he says nothing, doesn't even see them really. He seems to be worrying a puzzle he can't understand.

Then he leaves for Seattle.

Mother looks after the store, and there isn't a word, not a word, about Gary, about Cappy's grief, or about what might happen next.

Isn't anybody sad? Isn't anybody upset? I don't know Gary, don't know any of Cappy's children, but isn't it terrible, anyway? Something so terrible, you might want to cry and tear your hair and moan and lie on the bed and ask God why? But that's not the way Cappy behaved. And Mother doesn't say anything.

I know better than to bring it up. She has already told me over and over, "You're too sensitive, Billie," "You take things too seriously," "You can't carry the world on your shoulders." Or—as when I cried when the malamute was shot—"What's wrong with you?"

Clearly, there is something wrong with me for having these feelings when no one else does—not Mother, not Cappy, certainly not Lillian. Is it because I am "weak" like my father? Did I inherit this terrible flaw that makes me feel bad, scared, upset, when there is nothing to be scared of, nothing to feel bad about, as Mother tells me? And, even if things are bad, like, surely, Gary being gone is bad, then, that's life, she says, and you can't cry about it, because there's nothing you can do about it. Didn't she have to go through a lot—plenty—she says, more than her share? But there's no use complaining and there's no use feeling sorry for yourself. That's life.

So Mother says nothing. But she must have a lot of time to think. Standing there alone behind the counter, day after day. The three of us eating by ourselves in the kitchen in back of the store, returning to old man Lowenstein's house every night. She has plenty of time to think.

Maybe she speculates that Cappy won't, can't leave his wife now. Not now, not after they have lost a son. If there ever had been a time when he could have made a break, that time has passed.

It must have been a bitter realization. Where was she now? Back where she started, alone, with two children. I heard her anger years later, expressed in generalizations. How men string you along, waste your time, how they just take what they want without regard for you, for you, the woman.

She must have made her plans then. Thought about her options.

It is spring by the time Cappy returns. But soon afterward Mother tells us her decision. We are leaving Nome. Again.

This time, though, we are going back to San Francisco.

We're going to get out of here, she says. Like it is a good thing, something to celebrate, going back to San Francisco. Where you can see flowers once in a while, and trees and, most of all, where there's some sunshine. She is tired of the freezing cold and of the goddamn wind that never stops blowing.

And we'll be able to get fresh fruit, fresh fruit whenever we want it. And see some movies that aren't five years old. And get in a car and drive someplace. Imagine that! We'll go back to Golden Gate Park. Remember that? Remember "Portals of the Past"? Remember the Fun House?

The Depression is over. Things are good now. It won't be like it was before.

No, we aren't going to be stuck, like everybody else in Nome. That's what happens to people. They come up here thinking they're going to make their grubstake and get out, and then they just get stuck here forever. Stuck until it's too late to make a change. But not us. We are leaving, getting out of this ugly, miserable town for good.

She never says that it's over with Cappy. That he will never be our father. That he has let her down, strung her along. How can she say that, anyway, since the hope, the love, has never been acknowledged? It can't be over if it never existed.

Part of me buys my mother's pitch. It is good to go, good to move. It takes gumption, courage. I can look forward to the excitement of a big city, of a big school. Who wants to be in a rut, anyway?

But the warm scent of sourdough pancakes in Cappy's kitchen, the sight of his smug contentment with the rows of shiny bottles, the gentle slap—the constant, steady rhythm—of the breakers on the shore, even the repetitive, boring, hearty greetings emitted in steamy white breaths from the townsfolk on Front Street—all of these have become the sheltering walls of my existence.

But even if I were able to articulate these feelings, I wouldn't. It would be admitting that I am different than she is, feel differently than she does. If I say that it has been better in this dreary, homely place, better than it was before, that it would make me sad to leave, then I would be feeling sorry for myself. And I know, with a fearful certainty, that, in my mother's eyes, that would be committing the worst sin of all.

So, if I think about Cappy, about Fancy Andy and Russian Mike, or call to mind movies at the Dream Theatre, dancing under colored crepe-paper streamers at the gym—I don't acknowledge it. Maybe I can still hear the Bering Sea, hear the endless wash of breakers against the shore or the silence of the ice desert. If I do, I keep my feelings to myself.

FIFTY-SIX

We have no belongings to speak of—no furniture, few mementos, nothing to leave behind, nothing to ship. Mother doesn't collect things. Has never bought a piece of furniture or a set of dishes, has no cherished possessions. We leave Nome carrying one suitcase apiece.

It's good to travel light, my mother would say. Just as

she would say it's better not to need anybody, because, in the end, everybody lets you down.

It isn't easy to find a place to live in San Francisco. It is wartime. Apartments are scarce. But Mother manages to locate one on Albion Street, in the Mission District. Not a good neighborhood in these days. It's where the Mexicans live.

It is a typical old San Francisco flat, with its own entrance onto the street and, inside, a steep flight of stairs ending in a hallway. The rooms off that hallway are large and sunny, except for the kitchen, where the windows face the rear.

Besides the living room, with its bow window, a dining room, and kitchen, there are two bedrooms. The one between the living room and dining room can be closed off with sliding wooden doors. That becomes Lillian's room. Mother and I share the other bedroom, which is at the end of the hallway facing Albion Street.

As a condition of renting the flat, she had to agree to buy all the furniture left by the old couple who had lived there for twenty years. Apparently, they don't want any of it. Not the heavy mahogany table or the chairs with upholstered seats, not the dun-colored mohair sofa in the living room nor the glossy floor-model radio. They leave the upright piano and its bench full of old sheet music, the dark taffeta bedspreads and fringed throw pillows and the chinaware decorated with delicate floral wreaths that fill the glass-doored cabinets in the dining room. They even leave Bing, their canary.

They are retiring south of the Peninsula to San Jose, where it is warmer, sunnier, and where everything, I guess, will be new.

The furniture must have been lovingly cared for, because, though it is old, it shows little wear. An aura of endurance, propriety, and domestic contentment clings to the rooms.

Mother gets a job at the post office, sorting packages on the night shift. She doesn't like it. She's bored, and she doesn't care to see herself as a lowly civil service wage earner. Besides, the work is hard. Standing on her feet for eight hours, flinging packages. She isn't used to that kind of labor anymore. And she isn't a kid, anymore, either. She's forty-seven. But it's the best she can do.

I see her only on weekends.

Lillian can type and take shorthand like a whiz, and she is hired by the National Labor Relations Board. Every day she rides a bus to the cream-colored Merchandise Mart on Market Street, wearing pumps with Cuban heels, trim wool suits with jewel-neckline blouses, and little round hats that fit within the circle left by the roll of hair she wears tucked around a "rat." Although she would prefer to be simply a full-time stenographer and not a student, every evening after work she attends extension school to complete her senior year of high school. So I rarely see her, either.

I am a sophomore at Mission High, lost amid 2,000 strangers. I go to classes, pay attention, get A's, yearn for the notice of a devastatingly handsome blond boy in my

English class, and come home every afternoon to the empty flat on Albion Street.

There in the dim, high-ceilinged kitchen, I make a liverwurst sandwich (there is meat rationing, but you don't need coupons for liverwurst) and carry it into the dining room, where I let Bing out of his cage. He circles the room a few times, as if to test his wings after his long confinement, and then he flutters up to the molding near the ceiling, where he perches, occasionally emitting a faint *cheep* before dropping a small white deposit on the sideboard below.

I sit at the massive table, eat my sandwich, and then open my Official Gregg shorthand textbook and my Official Gregg shorthand notebook and spend a couple of hours practicing the new short forms I've learned in class that day.

There is something satisfying about seeing the perfectly shaped symbols marching evenly across the pale green lines, the circles and diagonal strokes filling page after page. For an hour or two I forget the empty, glaring streets outside the flat, and the tawdry shops along Mission, with their windows full of dusty displays of cheap merchandise, reminding me of my parents' failed businesses.

But when I have finished practicing my shorthand, or have tired of it, or have become aware all at once of myself alone in these rooms that look and smell and feel like someone else's, however benevolent the spirit they've left behind, there is this falling away in my chest, and I close my Official Gregg shorthand textbook and Gregg shorthand notebook and wander into the living room, where I sit at the piano, searching through the songbooks for something simple enough for me to pick out the notes of the treble part, and then I sing, to my own hesitant accompaniment, the words to old love songs giving expression to feelings I can't name.

Lillian must have come home before I go to bed, but I don't recall our spending time together. Maybe she is too exhausted after work and school, too busy getting her clothes ready for the next morning to do anything with me in the evenings.

It isn't until I lie alone in the double bed that the old couple had shared for so many years that I feel the full weight of my loneliness. I get up and crouch by the window and, like a spy, peep through the narrow space between the lowered shade and the windowsill.

Albion Street is a short residential block of old San Francisco flats such as ours, and there are few people outside after dark. It is like an empty stage set, its shadows punctuated by bright circles of light from the street lamps.

Somewhere beyond these dim pavements, far away downtown, my mother stands amid canvas bins, stands beneath bright fluorescent lights, in her gray striped skirt and vest and practical shoes that lace up and support the tiny feet she is so proud of. She seems as distant, in a place as remote and unknowable to me as she had years earlier, when I had waited for her to come home to that apartment on Sutter Street.

Beneath me, out the bedroom window, only the drunks, dispossessed when the bars along Mission close, venture onto my stage. I welcome their presence when they lurch unevenly into my view, intermittently visible in the circles of light, looking like wounded soldiers stumbling away from the battlefield, staggering toward safety.

Sometimes there are two of them, a man and a woman, clutching each other, their voices loud, too loud for the deserted street, and my heart beats faster as I watch them fall against each other in a doorway, where they become entangled and, peering between shade and sill, I strain to see their fumbling and merging, strain to understand what is happening in the shadows of the doorway. Somehow I understand what a low form of love this is. Yet I respond to their groping and searching, their helpless stumbling toward connection.

I am usually asleep by the time my mother comes home.

On Sundays the three of us take the streetcar to a cheap, second-run movie house on Market. It's a place for lonely people. People who will spend four or five hours in dark anonymity. Two films and a newsreel and short subjects. Between the two films, the overhead lights come on, exposing the slumped and silent figures, the empty seats and littered floor. Now the screen is hidden by a once-grand velvet curtain—gone the sleek and perfect movie faces, the glamorous rooms of white furniture, the polished nightclub floors mirroring the dancers' leaps and glides. Without warning, the make-believe is shattered, and there you are—exposed, reminded all at once of the lonely city, reminded of yourself and all too aware of the strangers around you.

And then a man, no longer young—maybe he had had ambitions once, maybe he had been a singer or a comedian, small-time, surely—this man, in a tuxedo, heavily made-up, smiling a broad, false, show-business smile, pushes a large, garishly colored wheel onto the stage. "Watch your numbers, folks—watch the wheel," he says, the smile never dimming. "You could be a winner today. This might be your lucky day."

Mother clutches her ticket stubs, watches the wheel, checks the numbers on her stub. She is oblivious of the terrible dreariness around her. She has laughed at the movie, eating her candy bar, and now is engrossed in the game. How can it be that her chest doesn't ache from the strangeness and loneliness as mine does?

There has not been a backward glance from her, not a word of regret or longing. What is wrong with me, then, that I feel this disconnectedness, this hollow yearning for I don't know what?

We know no one except Norma. She lives in a small apartment on Post Street, on the steep slant of a hill, and is working for the phone company again.

We go out together, just Norma and I, one day. Like the old days at Taylor Creek. Maybe. Norma wants to take me swimming. Though I don't swim, have never learned. She will teach me. It's easy, she says. Nothing to it.

I buy a bathing suit, a yellow two-piece, at one of the shoddy little stores on Mission Street.

Norma is a member of a swimming club at the Marina. She wears the black tank suit of a professional swimmer, a rubber swimming cap. And, though it is winter in San Francisco, there are old men who, like Norma, swim every day. And, like her, they are almost black from exposure to the sun, and their skin sags over still-hard muscles.

We stand next to each other in waist-high water and she tells me to just lie back, don't worry, she won't let me drown. I do as she tells me and she puts her hand under my back but I feel terrified and helpless. I thrash frantically, gulp water, panic.

Norma lets me go and I sit on a pier waiting for her. Feeling shamed, out of place and exposed in my two-piece bathing suit among the old men.

Afterward, we go to her apartment. Norma, in a long bathrobe, stands at a sideboard pouring a drink, while I sit waiting. She turns her head and looks at me over her shoulder for a long moment. Then, slowly, intentionally, looking steadily into my eyes, she lets her bathrobe slip to the floor and she is naked.

It is a fearful moment; I am paralyzed in my chair. Then it is over. She lifts her robe, nothing is said and it is over.

FIFTY-SEVEN

Eventually, I make a friend at Mission High. Cherie Sinclair. A skinny girl with thin blond hair, bowed legs, no eyebrows, no breasts, and a prominent nose. She draws dark arches over her eyes, wears falsies, and paints her thick lips with bright red lipstick.

I am shocked when she tells me that she and her mother go out on double dates and pretend to be sisters.

Cherie introduces me to the El Patio, a dance hall on Market Street where a large mirrored ball revolves above the floor, strewing shards of light over the dancers below. There are a lot of sailors at the El Patio and a lot of girls like Cherie and me.

I dance with the sailors, enjoying the feel of their flesh compressed under tight wool middies, the slick way their shiny black shoes glide across the El Patio floor. But my mother has told me, no dates with sailors. I may dance with them at the El Patio, but that's all.

But at least once she relents, and I have a date with a sailor. He is tall, I remember, and has a Brooklyn accent. We ride the streetcar to Ocean Beach and stroll along the chilly promenade, struggling to find something to talk about. I look out at the beach, sodden under an overcast sky, at the flat, sluggish ocean, at the black forms slithering over Seal Rock. We pass the life-size Gypsy doll, rocking back and forth and laughing in the window at the Fun House, and I feel something akin to fear, but more likely a sense of my own alienation as well as that of the mute stranger walking beside me, his fists curled into his pea-coat pockets.

Toward spring, after several grading periods, my home-room teacher is surprised to find that she has an all-A student in her class and begins to take an interest in me. She tells me that I am eligible to join the California Scholarship Association.

I go to a meeting of that group in a large lecture hall, and one of the girls with a beautiful soprano voice sings "They Wouldn't Believe Me." It is the first time I hear what I take to be classical music, and, all at once, I understand that there is a higher order in life, about which I know nothing.

I don't have a chance to find out what that might be, however, because school is about to let out and, when it does, we are going back to Nome.

FIFTY-EIGHT

Maybe my mother had been reminded of what she had forgotten—that San Francisco was a jinxed city. Maybe, after all, the ghosts of the past had defeated her, had made a new start impossible. Impossible, at least there, in that city whose beauty is only for those who haven't felt the loneliness at its center.

But that's not what she says. She would never say such

words out loud, probably never say them to herself, either. She can't afford to. Can't afford to be frightened. Can't afford to be overwhelmed. Can't afford despair.

No, what she says is that the post office is a dead end. That she won't be tied down, satisfied with routine like other people. Don't let the grass grow under your feet, she says. It's good to move, to make changes, to look for something better. That's how she puts it.

The post office is a dead end. We'll go back to Nome, where there's at least a chance of "getting ahead."

We'll leave the flat on Albion Street, the flat that was never ours, anyway—leave the heavy old furniture, the floral dishes, and taffeta bedspreads, the upright piano and, of course, leave poor Bing, abandoned to strangers once again.

For me, this place, this terrible, sad city, has never been, can never be, home. Never.

In Nome, there is little surprise at our return. No explanation is required. No one needs to ask what happened Outside, no one needs to ask about disappointment, about failure. No one, after all, comes back to Nome because they want to.

And, as usual, for Mother and for us, as well, there is no looking back. It is as if our year away had never happened. Just as those earlier years—years of my father's death, of Homewood Terrace and the Seattle Children's Home—had never occurred. We don't speak of it, of any of it, and, as time passes, it's not thought of, either. For us, as for many others here, memories are not to cherish, but to leave behind.

And Alaska, in its way, demands your full attention. Like a slap in the face, the assault of the weather, the landscape, the sheer physical effort of enduring, forces memories further and further away. And then the memories, at least for a child, become so faint, so intangible, as to make you wonder if they are memories, after all, or only dreams.

It will be years—a lifetime, really—before I understand the value of memories, before I grasp that they are, in fact, the essence of life, and before I try to reclaim them.

The town has changed in our year's absence. The war in Europe is over. The Japanese have retreated from the two islands in the Aleutians and no longer threaten imminent invasion. There is still an army base in Nome, but the tension, the sense of the town as a staging ground for major events, a stopover for dangerous or secret missions, has dissipated.

It appears that my mother has missed her chance at riding the wartime boom. Ironically, however, it is not the war but its end that will finally bring her the "opportunity" she has sought for so long.

Meanwhile, we return again to old man Lowenstein's house and to the liquor store and to Cappy. He is, finally, her only friend. The liquor store her only base. Whatever her disappointment, her sense of betrayal, even, she buries it in an attitude of good humor and stoical acceptance.

Nevertheless, perhaps she feels, as I do, that there is comfort in Cappy's welcome. He looks quizzically at my new short haircut, comments on how grown-up I am, shakes his head in mock disappointment that I am "too sophisticated" now to be his assistant. And he waves me to my accustomed seat among the boxes, saying he has been saving it for me, and he smiles as if he is glad I am there.

While the liquor store is once again my home base, the focus of my life has shifted. After all, now I am a teenager. Now I am a junior in high school. A junior!

The curriculum at Nome High fulfills the Territorial requirements—English, some math, and history. But it is heavy on "practical" courses such as home ec, typing, and bookkeeping. No one mentions college.

There is a new set of high school teachers every year, recommended by a Methodist board in Minnesota. Usually they're from the Midwest, from the farmlands of Iowa and North Dakota. They know about lives of work and hardship and about cruel winters and, except perhaps for Nome's stark isolation and desolate shabbiness, they're well prepared for what they find here.

Most of the women who come are verging on spinsterhood. Still a meaningful concept at this time. Still a dreaded fate. But inevitably, they will find what they have traveled so far seeking, they'll be married within a year. And, generally, that's the end of their teaching careers.

Like Miss Sprague. She hardly seems like a "spinster"—

she is perky and cute—but she might be thirty. She doesn't appear to mind the smelly school, the brutal and endless winter, or anything else about Nome. So it isn't a surprise when she marries one of the Fallon boys—Pete—whose whole large family, to a person, is cheerful, friendly, and energetic. She seems like one of them.

Miss Lovett, on the other hand, is austere and ungainly and looks as if she has been disappointed too many times. But she, too, is married within a year, to one of the mining engineers at The Company.

Invariably, the school principals are male, but they, too, often stay no more than one winter. During this, my junior year, Mr. Chapman holds the position, having spent his previous year as principal of the school in Sitka. Even with my limited perspective, I can understand that, remote and obscure as Sitka might be, Nome does not represent a step up. In fact, as far as professional ambition is concerned, this town is probably the end of the line.

Mr. Chapman is a heavy, shabby man and the bagged-out dark blue suit he wears every day is so shiny that when he turns his back to write on the blackboard, Vivian Rugg, the class jokester, whips out her comb and pretends to use the seat of his pants as a mirror.

Besides his duties as principal, Mr. Chapman teaches one or two classes. In the physics class he often seems more puzzled by the material than we are.

On the other hand, Max Beberman, who teaches during my senior year, is a gift. A fleshy, curly haired Jew from

Chicago, he has been stationed with the army in Nome and decides, just for a lark, I imagine, to take his discharge here and stay on for a while and teach.

He is the brightest moment in my school years. A brilliant mathematician from Chicago, he inspires in me a fondness for algebra. Later, after he returned to Chicago, he was credited with developing the "new math." At Nome High, Mr. Beberman amuses himself with some quiet jokes at our expense. He tells us, for example, that the suit he wears is a "shmatte," a Latin word meaning "fine wool," he explains, writing it carefully on the blackboard. My mother, who, of course, understands Yiddish, has some good laughs when I report on Mr. Beberman's language lessons.

One of the few teachers who stay on in Nome, other than the women who find husbands, is Arne Swenson. But then, Mr. Swenson seems to us to be from another planet. He is unswervably sweet-tempered, even in the face of ridicule and impertinence from the students, who lob paper airplanes and spitballs at him while he stands, eager and round-eyed, trying to share with us the wonder of the heavens by using some sort of a homemade star-charting device, consisting of a board with a string and chalk attached.

Mr. Swenson is a bachelor and, as with so many others in town, his earlier life, before Nome, that is, is a mystery. But, whatever his past, he seems wholly innocent and good and keen to immerse himself in the life of the school and of Nome. When he first appears in town, he wears a well-cut tweed coat and cap, but shortly after his arrival he buys a fur parka and mukluks. Then, every morning before school, he can be observed, his beatific face framed in a wolverine ruff, jogging around the periphery of the village, no matter how searingly brutal the weather.

"Crazy" is the general reaction around town.

FIFTY-NINE

While I had been a nonentity at Mission High, here, among Nome High's population of thirty-five students, I am a member of an elite triumvirate, one of three white girls in my class.

Nancy Cook, Vivian Rugg, and I strive to be "normal" teenagers—that is, to act and dress like the examples we see in the popular magazines. Nancy has a placid temperament and a round-faced, brown-eyed, brown-haired prettiness; Vivian is a tall, large-boned clown, and very smart.

We don't perceive living on a frontier as an adventure or an opportunity. Nor do we even consider the possibility of trying to learn about the Eskimo culture, even though at least half of our fellow students are Eskimo or part Eskimo. No, we try to distance ourselves from all of that. We don't want to identify with Nome, with this desolate outpost on the edge of the wilderness, and certainly not with

Eskimos, who are the farthest thing from fashionable that we can imagine. On the contrary, these are conditions to be overcome. They stand in the way of our being able to emulate exactly the image of teenage style we find in the sleek pages of *Life, Mademoiselle,* and *Seventeen.*

We spurn parkas and mukluks. We wear down-filled coats and sheepskin-lined boots. We send off for matching clothes—"sloppy joe" sweaters and pleated checked skirts; spend hours every night setting our hair in pin curls; hang out at a booth in the Nevada, drinking Cokes, giggling wildly at our own "in" references, and flirting with soldiers. We start a mimeographed school paper, run a contest for "best-dressed student," vote ourselves the winners. We even form our own three-member club, name ourselves "The Freelancers," and have official membership cards printed, although no one else is invited to join.

Nancy and Vivian have regular families, with mothers who stay home and keep house and dads who work in the gold-mining industry. Nancy's dad has his own mining outfit in the Kougarok, and Vivian's works for The Company—which, in addition to its three gold dredges and a dark, rickety wooden office building, even has a few homes for the families of major employees like the Ruggs.

Neither Nancy nor Vivian ever says anything about my mother's arrangement with Cappy. At least not to me. For the first time, though, I make comparisons. All I have known up until now is what I have sensed or guessed of the secret, puzzling bond that had existed between Cappy

and Mother. That and an image of marriage pieced together from my mother's bitter recollections of that distant, hateful joining with my father.

Now I watch my friends' parents in their homes, watch
the way they are together. Vivian's mom is buxom and
thin-legged, with upswept gray hair and a lively, sweet-
natured expression. Her dad's dark, lined face doesn't
often break open in a smile, but he has a deadpan kind of
humor that makes Mrs. Rugg laugh.

Even when they are standing across a room from each
other, there seems to be an invisible connection between
them.

And there is something about the way Mrs. Rugg says
her husband's name, as if she likes to say it, likes the
sound of it, as if it were an endearment, almost, and as if
he knows it, too.

Nancy's parents are older—older, it seems, than the
Ruggs, older than Mother and Cappy. We come upon
them in their living room one day, where the darkness has
taken over and no lamps are lit. They are sitting on their
couch, the old couple. And—like their living room, like
their furniture—they seem well-worn. Mrs. Cook, so
fleshy, her coarse gray hair carelessly pinned away from
her face, no makeup. Her body heavy, sagging into a
shapeless wedge of flesh under a loose housedress. Aged
and unadorned. The old man stiff and lean as a plank,
inward-turning. They sit close together in the darkened
room, their bodies touching, a knitted throw over their
knees.

The air in that room is heavy with intimacy, with the startled feel of intimacy interrupted.

Yet there are no embarrassed words or moves. Nothing, apparently, is unusual. And in that second, in that instant, in that closeness perceived, I understand that there can exist between a man and a woman something that isn't shameful and disguised. Something, perhaps, that is sweet, mysterious, and enduring.

SIXTY

Lillian is getting married. She, who never goes out on dates. All that time during the war when there were so many men, so many men hungry, desperate for women. When she could have had her choice. She never seemed to look up from the book that she was reading. I felt bad about going out with soldiers all the time, felt sorry walking out the front door and leaving her there alone with Mother. But I didn't know how to talk to her, to ask why. There was no way to ask Lillian things like that. She'd just look away and smile an awkward, half-embarrassed, half-annoyed smile, like she'd forgive you for your question, but she wished you'd leave her alone.

My sister wore glasses, had worn glasses since we were little and she read all the time when she wasn't sitting on Mother's lap, her arms around her neck. Not that she was studious. She didn't care about school. She didn't care about getting good grades.

For a while she had talked about going to secretarial college—in Chicago. There was a special school—the Gregg School—founded by the people who had invented that shorthand technique. She could learn to use a steno-type machine and be a court reporter. It was a hope. Or a dream, maybe. It never happened. But she did get the best secretarial job in Nome. Secretary to Mr. Grant, the president of the Miners and Merchants Bank.

When she puts on her nice wool suit, earrings, and a jewel-neckline blouse, it's as if she knows who she is, knows where she belongs in the world. She carries a long envelope bag under her arm. Taller in her high-heeled pumps, she stands up straight and looks ahead. She is a stenographer, she is a secretary. That's who she is.

She calls me "Sissy"; she always has. It was my sister who had said "Don't cry," as we waited for Mother in the dark apartment on Sutter Street, my sister who said Mother would be home soon. It was my sister who, in the picture from Homewood Terrace, is there, with her arm around my shoulder.

She was with me on that sunny day in San Francisco, the day we found my father, found him on the kitchen floor. She was with me in Homewood Terrace, in Cottage 24, with Mrs. Gans. She is the only one who can confirm for me that there really was a place called the Seattle Children's Home, when otherwise it would have no more substance than a dream. And on board the First Boat it had been Lillian lying in the bunk below me whose noisy breathing and gasping reassured me during the nightmare of that journey to Nome.

She had been there, but she never speaks of it, never speaks about any of it.

And because of her silence, I didn't hear the truth for many, many years. When she finally could talk about it, what she tells me is that she remembers none of it, not the Sutter Street apartment, not Homewood, not the Seattle Children's Home nor the long, horrible boat trip. She hardly even remembers Taylor Creek and the roadhouse. What she says, in fact, is that she has no memory of her childhood at all.

And so I realize that I was alone. For if she remembers none of it, then, in a way, she wasn't really there, and so there's no one, no one in this whole world, who can tell me if it is true, no one who can tell me if I remember things the way they really happened.

And now she is going to be married! To Smitty. A scrawny little guy with a big nose, thin sandy hair. He has a job with Nome Telephone, a lineman. Smitty is one of those men who just show up in town all of a sudden, men with no past, with one or two skills they can use to get a job. They fit right in, these strangers with no past, laugh and joke with the locals like they've always been here.

How did this happen? Has she been seeing him, going out with him—to the movies? Or for rides in the telephone company truck? Wouldn't I have noticed? Wouldn't somebody—one of my girlfriends—have noticed and said something? Maybe she knows him only from the bank, when he comes in to do business at the bank. Maybe he flirts with her there. He has a big smile.

Probably they don't know each other very well, Smitty and Lillian. Probably she has no idea what you're supposed to feel about a man when you decide to marry him. I can't imagine that she has learned any more from Mother than I have—that is, any understanding of what it feels like to be in love, what it means to love a man or to be loved, for that matter.

Still, I'm glad my sister will have somebody for herself, her own man. But I don't much like Smitty. Mother doesn't, either. He smiles too much. And there is too much he doesn't say.

Nevertheless, while my mother might not consider him the most desirable of sons-in-law, she thinks it proper and appropriate that Lillian get married. There is no conflict in her mind between the picture she has drawn for us in anecdotes and memories of marriage as burdensome at best, childbearing as unspeakable agony, child rearing as self-sacrifice, and her acceptance of the conventional attitude that a girl is a failure if she doesn't manage to snare a man.

Lillian sets the date—sends away for a wedding dress and a veil. And she has this serene look on her face. A look I've never seen before. What can anyone do?

Except it turns out they can't get married on that date, because Smitty is already married. To somebody back in the States. One of the things he hasn't mentioned. Lillian doesn't say anything about it; she waits a while and sets another date.

And then they are finally married in the Federated Church with the minister reading the service. And Mother wearing a black velvet dress with little rhinestones around the collar and Smitty's thin hair slicked back with some kind of oil, making his nose appear even larger, and we have our pictures taken, all of us together on the plank sidewalk, standing in front of our shabby frame house, Lillian in her satin dress with the veil blowing behind her, gazing down, a little smile on her face, looking shy or maybe dreamy, or maybe not really there at all.

It didn't last long, that marriage. Long enough, though, for Lillian to have a son, to become a mother. There would be another brief marriage, two more children, and then she would have what—it seems now—she must always have wanted: someone to take care of. As she had taken care of me. To care for, as she, herself, had never been cared for. It was as if that was why she had survived.

SIXTY-ONE

When the army announces an auction of "surplus" clothing and matériel, my mother sees her opportunity. She will make a bid.

Before she does, however, she has a conversation with
a sergeant who happens to stop by the liquor store. Turns
out, he also happens to be in the Quartermaster Corps
and knows something about the upcoming auction, and,
in fact, he has access to the secret bids. Maybe he would
be willing to share the information with her. For a con-
sideration.

Overnight, my mother is in business. The surplus business. Crates and crates of fliers' clothing, sheepskin-lined
leather pants, jackets, and even helmets. All for pennies a
pound. Furthermore, she has bought a place to put them.
A former army prophylactic station, it is a tiny shell of a
building with no heat or windows. But it is right on Front
Street, on a lot two doors down from the liquor store.

Wearing her plaid lumber jacket, her tiny hands encased in rough canvas gloves, my mother goes to work pry-
ing open the wooden crates with a claw hammer, singing
"Red Sails in the Sunset" in her small, sweet voice, her
breath leaving white clouds in the air.

Once the cases are open, she pulls out a magazine,
leans against a crate and waits for customers. She doesn't
need many, she explains—wanting to talk about it, wanting to share her excitement at the windfall. Charging ten
or fifteen dollars for a jacket that has cost her a few
cents, she need sell only two or three a day to make a
good living.

So she waits patiently, stands reading under the single
bulb, the sharp bones of her face etched by the overhead
light, oblivious to discomfort, to the long hours alone, the

cold, bare room. No windows, nothing to look at but the raw, unfinished walls, the piles of used clothing. What of it? she would say. Why should it bother her? This was her chance. Her big chance. At last.

And the customers come. At long intervals. Maybe only five or six the whole day. Where else can they get clothing like this in Nome? Made from the best materials. And for so little. Mother at last has her break—a foothold, a chance to back away from the edge of failure and despair.

What I haven't noticed—yet how is it possible?—is that our life with Cappy is over. Over. Mother has her own business now. We're still living in Cappy's father's house, but she doesn't have time to clerk in the liquor store, she doesn't have time to cook. Of course.

As usual, nothing is said. Not a word. She doesn't mention Cappy. Doesn't stop by his store to say hello, nor does he drop by her place.

I don't have to be told not to ask. Cappy is obliterated as completely as my father was. Except I can still see him, still see the liquor store. Right there on Front Street.

Had there been some final break? Some final expectation not realized? I can't believe that Mother had held onto her hopes after all that had gone before. But now it seems, in an act of complete rejection, she has simply given in to her anger, her sense of being wronged.

Still, when I visit, stop by the liquor store, Cappy smiles and nods to me, beckoning me in as if nothing has changed, as if I am expected. He asks, "How's your mother doing?" So casual, as if he has no more interest than that, as if there'd been no more connection than that. It seems that he is capable of endlessly keeping up a façade. Cheerfulness, casualness, innocence.

Or had I made it all up? Again? Imagined that she had once shyly asked if I wanted him as my father, imagined that we had sat down to meals together like a family, the four of us together night after night?

Now, when I start to leave, Cappy says, "Where you going?" Tells me to go back to the kitchen and fix myself a sandwich. Hang around. Where am I rushing off to?

But the kitchen reverberates with our absence—an empty place, now, where Mother had stood day after day at the big black range, bending over the oven basting the sizzling reindeer roast with a big metal spoon, Cappy's lips curling in anticipation of the oozing red meat. That's enough, that's enough, Rose, he'd say—don't overcook it. And Mother tolerant, good-natured, competent, sure of herself. Now the range is tepid, with only the memory of warm aromas clinging to the cold air. The windows frame the heavy stillness of the frozen sea.

Meanwhile, in the liquor store, Cappy stands alone behind the counter. The shadows deepen, and he waits, as always, waits with his hand on the string, waits to pull the light, waits until it is almost too dark to see.

SIXTY-TWO

At four o'clock each afternoon, Corporal Wendell Weninger sits waiting for me outside the school, waiting behind the wheel of an army truck to drive me to my job as a clerk at the PX. Wendell has a round, smooth face, round blue eyes, a pink, bud-shaped mouth, and a slight lisp. Bouncing along on the road to the base, he recites his plan to kill the lieutenant. "One of these dayths I'm going to drive thith truck right into a pole," he says, "—right into a pole and thmash that prickth's head."

The PX is half of a Quonset hut, the other half given over to a snack bar run by two privates named Pedro I and Pedro II. I work from four in the afternoon until nine at night, and all day Saturday. When things aren't busy, Wendell and I neck in a little storage room at the end of the U-shaped counter.

Saturday mornings are my favorite time at the PX. I open up at eight, and, before the customers come, maybe for an hour or so, it's my private realm, warm and quiet and cozy. I sit behind the counter, my rear end wedged onto a shelf and my feet braced against an opposite shelf under the counter, and I open a package of Lorna Doones and a can of orange juice and sit there savoring the crumbly sweetness of the shortbread and the tinny bite of the juice, the two Pedros chattering on the other side of the thin wall, a dim background to my dreamy state. I feel safe, as in Homewood, safe in a secret hiding place.

Meanwhile, at school, the principal sends for me and for Walter McCarthy. We are the two best students. He has selected us, he says, to take the Pepsi-Cola scholarship test.

The soft-drink company is offering full college scholarships—two for each state in the union and one each for the territories of Hawaii and Alaska—to the best high school seniors.

I take the test even though college isn't in my plans. The only plan I have is to be a secretary like my sister. To wear nice wool suits and high-heeled pumps and sit at a big shiny desk in an office with a carpet on the floor.

That's not altogether true. I have a fantasy, although it is hardly a plan. In the fantasy, I am Rosalind Russell. Not Rosalind Russell the movie actress, but Rosalind Russell the ace newspaper reporter in *His Girl Friday*—banging out a scoop on an old typewriter, cigarette dangling from the side of my mouth (I'd have to learn to smoke), hat jammed lopsided on my head, good-looking, wisecracking fellow reporters on every side.

That's my fantasy, born completely of the movies. To be a reporter. In a big city. To be where things are happening, exciting things, to be *part* of what is happening. My dream, in short, is to be in a place that is the exact opposite of where I am now.

Somewhere, too, another rankling of ambition, of change, has been set in motion, although its larger meaning, its implications, are beyond me. It has come about—

this vague, restless feeling of quest—because of Sinclair Lewis's *Main Street.* His quintessential description of small-town life is a revelation, for in it I recognize Nome, which, for all its exotic qualities, is defined, too, by the narrowness and limitations of small-town America. And, perhaps more crucially, I begin to discern, vaguely, tentatively, that somewhere there exists a world where the accepted language is the one that Sinclair Lewis speaks—a language of ideas and, even, of feelings.

But it isn't until I receive the letter from Pepsi-Cola, the letter informing me that I am a finalist, the letter suggesting I apply to the college of my choice—it isn't until I send away and receive the college application and the brochure with pictures of the avenue of tall palm trees leading to the sandstone quadrangle, see, almost feel, the pale, sun-warmed stones, see students beautiful as movie stars clutching books to their chests, faces turned up to the light—it is only then that I understand that this might be the door to that world I have just begun to perceive.

My mother is excited. Can you beat it? A daughter of mine going to college? Me, with no education, coming from the Old Country. That's America for you. What a country!

She sees it as her own accomplishment—one she hasn't even dreamed of. It has been enough, more than enough, that she has survived, an immigrant, a woman alone, a woman with two children, that she has kept us all from hunger, that she has kept a roof over our heads. Suddenly, she sees her achievement on a larger scale.

The second letter from Pepsi-Cola arrives one day while I am at school. My mother hands it to me when I come home for lunch. She never opens my mail, but she has opened this letter. She doesn't say anything. She just hands it to me with an expression I've never seen before. My mother looks apprehensive, frightened.

I haven't won. I won't get a scholarship. Instead there's an Honorable Mention and an award of fifty dollars.

My mother needn't have been afraid of my disappointment. I cry, but more from chagrin than sadness. Because I don't really understand what I have lost. My dreams haven't become fixed—they are such distant, elusive notions, anyway. It is hard to see myself in that other world, the shape and form of which I haven't yet imagined.

Or perhaps I have simply learned too well my mother's stoicism, her readiness to put aside dreams for what is present, possible, tangible. Dreams are fragile, evaporating easily. More important, they can hurt you, their loss leaving you weakened and helpless.

So, when an opportunity comes along soon afterward, I take it without hesitation. The lieutenant in charge of the PX offers me a full-time job in the office after I graduate. An office job! With the US Army! A job where I will sit down at a desk.

College isn't real. A job with the army is.

SIXTY-THREE

The PX office is on the second floor of an airplane hangar across the landing field from the PX store. It isn't much—small, bare, overheated, furnished with three square wooden desks and a few metal file cabinets. The staff consists of the lieutenant, his wife, and me.

Mrs. Lieutenant is plump and wears ill-fitting print dresses; her hair is in girlish long curls, and, whenever she has a chance, she brushes up against her husband or lets her hand fall on his shoulder or the back of his neck. He pretends to ignore her overtures, sitting stiffly at his desk, in his sharply creased uniform shirt, shiny silver bars on the collar, a pipe clenched between his teeth, fingering the endless pieces of paper that appear each day. Their desks are butted together, so that they face each other. My desk is wedged into a corner across the room.

My main assignment is "inventory control." That is, each day I enter in triplicate on 3 × 5 cards the numbers of Mounds bars or El Roi Tan cigars that were sold at the PX the previous day. Or I keep track of how many Zippo lighters or cartons of Camels have arrived at the warehouse. I slip each set of cards into a cellophane sleeve in a long leather binder.

I work in silence at my desk in the corner, carefully filling out the cards in my large, neat hand, aware of the steaming radiator, of the murmurs and byplay of the lieutenant and his wife across the room, my world confined to the 4' × 4' desk top, the bare plywood walls I face, and the narrow, leather books of 3" × 5" cards.

After work, I go to my mother's store. By now, she has moved her merchandise across the street to a real store—little more than a shack, really, but it has some shelves, a name, the Trading Post, and a big window overlooking Front Street. She has also bought a Quonset hut at auction, which is now attached to the rear of the store and serves as her warehouse. There, surrounded by the open cases, the cold air stale and unmoving, I keep her company for as long as I can stand it.

She bends over the boxes, absorbed with sorting through her treasures. Her face is set, intent. She considers each item, holding up a jacket, a pair of pants. Is it salable or not? If she decides it is, she folds it over the edge of the crate; if not, she tosses it on the floor.

To me, the wooden crates seem like caskets, the leather clothing like so many discarded skins. Hopelessly, I pick through the jackets, searching the names stamped in leather, looking for one that may call up a face, a voice, a moment. The sleeves are creased at the elbows, they bear the impression of arms that might have held me, of a boy who might have pressed his moist cheek against mine, a stranger with whom I'd shared a momentary intimacy, when we were connected to each other, to the music. They have been shed, sloughed off like molted skins, their wearers disbursed to lives far away, to mothers and girlfriends, to warm places where these aren't needed, the

time in Nome nothing more than a remote interlude, dis-
jointed, faint, forgotten.

Meanwhile, across the street, perhaps right now standing invisibly behind the dark reflection of his plate-glass
window, Cappy might be watching.

He is forgotten, too. No—he doesn't exist. Buried and
frozen in my mother's cold anger, whose source is never
made clear but ultimately I think is due to the dreams she
had allowed herself to have in spite of her cautious and
reasoning mind, which tells her dreams are dangerous.

I don't know when she finally set aside her hopes, but
my mother would never look back. This was it. This was
the end of the abrupt leavings, the mysterious returns.
Her quest is over. This shack, this makeshift store, with its
plywood shelves and musty, sour smell of used clothes,
the waves of dry heat from the oil burner, the view out to
the muddy stretch of Front Street, the sagging, weather-
worn buildings—this is the opportunity that has shaped
so much of our lives. To my mother, it is security, it is fortune, it is the future. To me it seems a prison—worse, soli-
tary confinement.

I don't recall the exact moment when I know I will
leave. Leave alone, leave for good. Perhaps it is during
those times when I watch my mother sifting through the
discarded uniforms. When I see her, contented, singing
softly as she works, and feel, in contrast, the crushing
dreariness of the scene around me.

Or perhaps it is on one of those mornings when I fight
my way across the shelterless landing strip between the PX

store and the hangar, bent into a ferocious wind, gasping as it tears my breath away, my brow, my cheeks, my chin stinging, then aching with the fierce cold, clutching the cigar box full of PX receipts to my chest, struggling toward the hanger and the office where I will spend the silent day with the lieutenant and his wife.

Or maybe the decision begins to form one morning, one like so many others, when I find myself crouched on a slapped-together wooden bench in the back of the army truck whose plywood cover converts it into a bus, huddled in the dark, hugging myself against the cold, the only passenger as the truck jolts along Front Street toward the base. Perhaps it is at the moment when I look out through the square hole cut in the plywood and see between Front Street's worn and battered buildings the cold sun inching up over the ice on the Bering Sea.

This morning the familiar view—the vast, barren white desert—is transformed. As I watch, long shafts of gold and pink appear, trembling along the crystalline snow cover. They ricochet off the spires of ice jutting from the pressure ridges, turning them into glittering obelisks, glinting fingers pointing up, up toward the sky.

It is as if for the first time I am aware of my own consciousness, of my own eyes looking out on the world—aware, in fact, of the feeling of wonder.

At that moment, I know, as surely as I know what I have just seen, that there are no words in this place with which to speak of it, no language for my feelings. And, while this understanding may not have framed itself so clearly for me at that exact moment, it is, nevertheless, my sense of this vision and of my own solitude that, as much as anything else, sends me on another journey. One that I will make alone.

SIXTY-FOUR

My mother doesn't ask me why, nor does she argue. Perhaps this is her dream, too. Perhaps she has only been waiting for me to speak.

"If you want to go to college, baby," she says, "we'll work it out somehow."

We talk about it, facing each other over the chest-high oil heater in the Trading Post. It looks like the surplus business is going to be a steady thing, she says. Besides, I have a few war bonds I can cash in; Lillian offers to give me what she can spare from her salary each month.

"Altogether," Mother says, "that should be enough to get you through one year. After that, we'll just see what happens."

I don't remember the day I leave Nome. Nor the long flight to Seattle. It would have been winter, it would have been snowy and bitter cold. But all that I recall is that my sister and mother wish me well and say that I am to write, write often. And that I leave alone, on my way to the campus with the sun-warmed stones.

You can always come back, Mother says.

But I won't. Not to live, not ever again.

*

Sometimes now I think of returning, of going back to see what has become of the Taylor Creek roadhouse. I understand that there is a road—passable, of course, only in the summer—and that you can drive from Nome to Taylor.

Maybe I will go back and drive that road to see what remains. Maybe I will walk the tundra and stand on the very spot where I stood before.

Maybe. But I don't think so. Maybe I'll just keep my memories.

ABOUT THE AUTHOR

JULIA SCULLY was born in Seattle and moved with her mother and sister to Alaska before the outbreak of World War II. She was valedicto-
rian of her class (of ten) at Nome High School, graduated from
Stanford, and came to New York. After jobs at *Argosy* and other publi-
cations, she became editor of *Modern Photography*. She has had count-
less articles on the art of photography published worldwide. She wrote
a weekly syndicated feature for the Associated Press and a bimonthly
column for the publication *Photography in New York*. She lives in Man-
hattan.

A NOTE ON THE TYPE

This book was set in Fairfield, the first typeface from the hand of the distinguished American artist and engraver Rudolph Ruzicka (1883–1978). Rudolph Ruzicka was born in Bohemia and came to America in 1894. He set up his own shop, devoted to wood engraving and printing, in New York in 1913 after a varied career working as a wood engraver, in photoengraving and banknote printing plants, and as an art director and freelance artist. He designed and illustrated many books, and was the creator of a considerable list of individual prints—wood engravings, line engravings on copper, and aquatints.

DATE DUE

JAN 0 5 1999	FEB 2 3 2005	
FEB 0 3 1999		
SEP 0 7 1999		
AUG 0 7 2000		
AG 2 '01		
AP 4 '02		
AP 27 '02		
JY 5 '02		
JE 12 03		

O 11/98
B 8/10

DEMCO